CAR

LOCKOUT BUSINESS

EMERGENCY LOCKSMITH SERVICE 24-7

UNLOCK CARS AND MAKE MONEY;

LOCKSMITH, LOCK AND KEY, LOST KEYS

AUTHOR, S. CORMIER

ISBN: 9781790421619

Published by:
aDuxpond Publishing

Warning & Disclaimer

This manual is designed to give the reader information on the "Quickly Make Money Opening Cars." This is the only startup business book you'll ever need, it is designed and intended help you get your business up and running in the least amount of effort and time. This book will help you with the basic functions of becoming a car opening, a business person, as well as where to buy tools, business tips and techniques and many secrets. It is sold with the understanding that the author and/or publisher are not engaged in rendering legal, accounting or other professional advice. If legal or other professional advice is required, the services of a competent person and/or company should be sought.

It is not the purpose of this manual to provide all the information on the subjects covered, but to emphasize many areas of business in which a beginner within the industry needs help. The purpose is to give a general background in the business aspects and touch on the needed information required to start a business. It is recommended that you read all the information that is available on this subject matter. This business is not a get-rich-quick scheme. It requires time, education and effort to become skilled in this or any career.

The author(s) and/or publisher(s) have written this to educate and entertain the reader. Therefore the author(s) and/or publisher(s) shall have neither liability, nor responsibility to any and all persons or entities with respect to any loss or damage caused directly or indirectly by the information contained in the book.

WHY YOU SHOULD READ THIS BOOK

If I only had a mentor to teach me the ropes and keep me from making the countless mistakes I have encountered over the years. If only there was a guide, a teacher or a personal aid to help me.

There were innumerable times I wished for a guidebook, a manual or even a pamphlet, but there was none. I needed this business handbook to get me through the tough parts of my career. I need this book at the beginning of my career... yes, in the beginning when I first started out. This insight took me over 20 years to see; when I look back I see it so clearly. Now I am giving you the years of experience that brought me from a starving young man trying to make his way, to a successful business man. This book that you now have in your hands will help you bypass what most people struggle through. You can get started today with this book full of knowledge and turn a dream into a successful and fun career. Remember; once you start you will be around for as many years as there are cars to drive.

I have helped many of my fellow car openings over the years. They kept expressing to me that a written copy of the knowledge, information and resources that I have learned the hard way, needs to be shared. By putting these documents into a book will provide a service to the car opening community that can be used over and over again. This book would be a valuable resource for the beginner as well as a seasoned pro. It would create an atmosphere of education and make the business portion of our trade easier. This would give them a reference in their needs now and in the future and be a great addition to their library.

Striking out on your own with a tool such as this book will not only balance the playing field, but tip the scales in your direction. It will give you the advantages that most people struggle with and save you many hours of frustration, plus stop any delays with your business success.

Many times I have spoken to the "newbie" young entrepreneur struggling to feed his family. You know this guy, his intentions are good and he would toil within his dead-end job for years. He would proudly work his fingers to the bone, and do this for low wages, all for someone he doesn't even like. Yet he is scared of the unknown, terrified of starting something new, we all are. Since the car opening industry is so secretive, most well intentioned folks never even try. BUT!!! Once they read the "Quickly Make Money Opening Cars" book, it will become clear that your J.O.B. (Just Over Broke) is not where you want to be. It is time to change careers, start out on your own, to create a better like for you and your family.

This book contains many easy steps that will guide you through the toughest learning parts of business. When you follow the steps and comprehend each part, it will bring you closer to your goal of becoming self-employed. These approaches are time tested and used every day within the car opening industry, by me and many other business people, it's how I do things on a day by day basis.

Believe in yourself… I believe in you and your passion to be a great business person, it's as easy as taking these 10 steps to success. Spend the time and continue reading, finish every step. You will become the business person you have always wanted to be.

If you are looking for a recession proof business with low overhead costs, the car opening business was made for you. When people are locked out of their cars, they are desperate, they must have them opened. In the event they do not have money to pay for your service, they will call friends, neighbors, relatives and even their insurance companies, all of these people will help them pay you. You always get paid, it's awesome!

Many of the instructions are of article length and are illustrated; you'll also discover new and unique ways to grind away business problems. If you are a beginner to the trade there are articles outlining recommended tools, articles addressing very basic business practices and clear most of the challenges you will see every day in your business career.

Unlike many of the car opening books published this book is over 150 pages of good information. This book gives insight and step-by-step processes to get into business and is time tested by a successful trade leader. This book includes business insights, tools and how to work smarter not harder. This is the most comprehensive book written; it covers the "meat and potatoes" and will help you get into this lucrative business.

Here is a quick slice of information about our trade: Did you know that you can sign up with major auto clubs to do their light duty roadside services such as retrieving keys lock inside cars, jump starting dead batteries in member's cars, even deliver gas. All this can be done right in your hometown, neighboring towns and counties. You just need to sign up on their website, they will call, then watch the money roll into your bank account.

Whether you are in need of a career change, have a desire to help others or just enjoy the freedom of being your own boss, this may be the opportunity you've been looking for!

Here is just a taste of the many available to you:

Good Sam Roadside Assistance
1-800-601-2850
Affinity Road & Travel Club, LLC and
Americas Road & Travel Club, Inc.
P.O. Box 6900
Englewood, CO 80155

GEICO
1-800-424-3426

Emergency Road Service
PO Box 8075
Macon, GA 31208-8075

AAA Colorado Headquarters
1-800-222-4357
4100 E. Arkansas Avenue
Denver, CO 80222

Top 10 Reasons Why You Should Read This Book

10. You want to learn the path that I took to go from nothing to free time, extra money and endless job.

9. You want to learn about the course of action that I took and the lessons I learned along the way.

8. You want to study from all the mistakes we made over the years so that your business can avoid making some of the same ones.

7. You want to figure out the right balance of profits, passion, and purpose in business and in life.

6. You want to build a long-term enduring business and brand.

5. You want to create a stronger company, which will make you happier and highly productive.

4. You want to deliver a better customer experience, which will make your customers happier and create more customer loyalty, leading to increased profits.

3. You want to build something special for you and your family.

2. You want to find inspiration and happiness in work and in life.

1. You ran out of firewood for your fireplace. This book makes for an excellent fire starter.

INTRODUCTION

If someone would have told me that it only took 10 simple and easy steps to be years ahead of my competitors, I would have spent the money on this book. Not only did I spend time repairing the honest, as well as stupid makes I made. There was years of trials and errors to overcome. They were honest slipups, in fact at the time I thought I was doing everything right. This book would have erased most if not all the mistakes.

Because of not having this book in the beginning, I put in the many hours, toiled, sweated and gave up numerous hours of sleep, yet my business thrives even as I write this. Yet, I still wonder how much better the profession I chose could have been with help from the information complied hear in the "Quickly Make Money Opening Cars" book. I call this a book but it is more representative of having a silent partner with the business knowledge that I lacked without even knowing.

At one point I started thinking about what characteristics are mutual among car openings. That's when he realized I could put my own business savvy and strong work ethic into starting and running my own lockout service.

A car opening is an exceedingly honest man. He has good habits and a keen sense of right and wrong. He cooperates with the police at all times and never divulges any of his secrets. If there is any doubt about the honesty of the customer or integrity of the job he stops the work immediately.

The car opening is honorable with a good reputation. He must preserve the confidence and trust that has been built up over many years. He must keep himself above suspicion at all times. The public has a high opinion of his profession so he must always act with integrity and use good judgment.

Right this very minute, someone, somewhere has locked their keys in their car. It happens every day, all day long and into the wee hours of the morning.

The cost of equipment is strikingly low; it requires a phone, vehicle and your time. You can start part time and do nights and weekend, and work the hours you want. There are service providers, such as AAA, Progressive Insurance, OnStar, State Farm, Geico, and just about every insurance company. Make a quick phone call to your insurance agent and let them know you're a lockout specialist, then sit back and watch the calls come your way.

If your wanting full time, spend a few minutes every day and sign up online to every "Emergency Road Service" provider you can find and they will keep you on the road every minute of every day.

You decide how much you want to work and how much money you want to make.

PURPOSE OF THIS MANUAL

The purpose of this manual is not to give you specific techniques on how to do car openings but to educate you on the backend processes to make you a successful in the car opening business. This book will teach you at least one surefire way to open a car in just minutes within this manual. You'll be taking a look into the business aspects and workings of turning a wish of being an entrepreneur into reality. The tools, method and suggestion you will receive in these chapters will open doors and create an environment of success, confidence and of course financial gain, through the knowledge and efforts of yourself with the guidance from within these pages.

This manual will step you through the hardest part of this profession, which is learning the business side of things, as well as the easiest ways to pop open a car door in seconds and there is no need to reinvent the wheel, it's all here. It has been done for you by knowing what works and what doesn't in the areas of advertising, communications, training, plus the business side of this industry and many more areas can make the difference between success and failure in this trade. That is why this book was written for you, the business person in this book, "Quickly Make Money Opening Cars" in 10 easy steps.

You have taken the very first step of a journey into more free time then you ever imagined more money and many lifelong friends that you will help you in your journey and guide you throughout the car opening industry. This step that you have just taken will give you a broader education and the business background that most people in this field will not give to their closes friend, no less you an individual that they do not know. Take the time to read this book and study the areas that are new to you, and keep it handy for the times that a quick refreshment or help with a question.

We had four goals for writing this book: first that these pages will serve as mentors for your business startup. Second, we trust that when you read these pages, you will be motivated to start a life long journey in business, of which should help you grow rich in your walk past your old life of working for the “Man”. Removing yourself from the 9 to 5 job and controlling you own destiny. Third, we hope this book will serve as a guide for becoming an independent person that will make your own occupation, trade or even a franchise. Finally, for those of you who are already in business, this guide is designed to direct you to further your education and knowledge and to introduce you to lesser-known ideas and thoughts that you may be unaware of.

This isn't just a book, it's an adventure story, a journey that you can join in and make completely your own. It's about how living with purpose can generate powerful benefits for you and the world around you.

Quick Story...

Not Quite Awake

One afternoon a car opening friend of mind and I went out to unlock a car. After a short drive, we got there and the customer was trying very hard with a clothes hanger, in which they jammed it between the door and the car body trying desperately to open the door before we arrived. I would like to have said they did no damage but that in its self would be a gross understatement. As we approached the car I pointed to the rear window on the passenger side. Trying very hard not to laugh we pointed out to the car owner that the window was rolled down. The hard part for the customer was paying the bill anyway. This is because we do not charge to open the car, we charge for the trip out to the job site.

TABLE OF CONTENT

CHAPTER ONE

Place to Start

It is always easier when there is a set of step (10 easy steps) to get your career started, don't wait start today.

This section will walk you through the entire manual in a step-by-step sequence to make it very easy for you to put all of the information to work for you very quickly.

CHAPTER TWO

Advertising

There is many ways to advertise and you could spend every dime you make, I am here to help you take control and minimize the advertising bandits. Put that money into your pocket not theirs. There are as many ways to spend in this area of business and only one way to keep it.

CHAPTER THREE

Communications

The old way, the new way and what is time tested. What mistakes I made so you won't.

CHAPTER FOUR

Insurances

From auto to workman's Comp and a little bonding in between, topics that are important for your protection.

CHAPTER FIVE

Training & Education

Many times we can be trained for little or no cost, yet there are times in which, a true classroom education in specialty areas of car opening are needed. The need to find books, videos, schools and even trade association are need, these and more are covered.

CHAPTER SIX

Paperwork

As with anything we do in life there is always paperwork that need to be completed. Attention to details will save you time and it's encouraged that you extract every ounce of information you can from this section.

CHAPTER SEVEN

Money Matters

Guidelines in how much to charge, forms of payment and pitfalls of taking the wrong types of payments.

CHAPTER EIGHT

Appearances

It is difficult to overestimate the importance of finding how you and your vehicle and signage can and will make your company succeed. Not one item within this chapter should be overlooked, your reputation needs to be at the of the peak performance.

CHAPTER NINE

Getting Business

The art of getting business is part finesse and part skill, this chapter give you a competent approach to dealing with the commonality that most of us have. It bridges the stages of ones lack of self-assurance to being a fulfilled business person.

CHAPTER TEN

Telephone Skills

Having the ability to do well on the phone is not a rare gift but a practiced talent that can be learned. Usually gained through training and educations, the most basics of these skills are here for your taking.

CHAPTER ELEVEN

The Law

It's said that ignorance is no excuse and that hold true to this industry. Don't go into this career without knowing the fundamentals and how it effects your decisions.

CHAPTER TWELVE

Tools

Basic Entry and Tools used within the industry.

Chapter One

Place to Start

This section will walk you through the entire manual in a step-by-step sequence to make it very easy for you to put all of the information to work for you very quickly.

The material in this manual has all you'll need to build a successful car opening business. You may already have ideas of your own that you believe would be good for your business but chances are that "I have already been there and done that!" I have over twenty five years of experience in the car opening business and will do my best to make you aware of all the tools, methods, skills and options available to you. I strongly suggest that you follow our recommendations first, and then experiment with other ideas after you become familiar and successful with the thoughts and ideas within this manual.

There are many small car opening businesses currently operating that are barely making enough money to pay their bills. "Don't become one of these failing companies. These establishments come and go every year, you will not with the help within this document. It is almost fun to look in the Yellow Pages each year just to see who is new and who is out of business. On the other side of the coin, there are some very successful car opening businesses out there, and some of them are even franchising their businesses nationwide. Why are some very successful and others are dwindling? I have quizzed, interviewed and spoken with some of the companies that are barely surviving (which we consider failing) as well as the most successful business out there. I have discovered that in each and every case the reason that they are falling (and the only reason they are failing) is that they do not have the information that you have in your hands right now! The most successful companies had one thing in common, information, the same information within this book.

Let's get started…

Make $60 to $85 by removing key that are locked inside your customer's cars and handing them to the owner!

STEP 1...

WHAT ARE GOING TO CALL YOURSELF

The very first thing that you need to do is to get into a position that will allow you to legally purchase and carry car opening tools. Car opening tools are not sold to just anyone and some cities have possession laws making them illegal unless you are in one of the accepted trades or businesses that are permitted to have them. You will need to meet the criteria which will place you in an accepted trade or business.

This can be done by deciding just what you want to be known as. I'm not talking about a business name, but more along the lines of what trade or type of business you are in. I strongly suggest that you call yourself a "Car Opening Expert" right from the start and here's why. The car opening industry is very hard to get into if you're not already a car opening expert. Sounds funny, doesn't it? Here's what I mean. Have you ever heard this before?

"I'm sorry I cannot hire you because you do not have any experience." It's a catch 22; you cannot get a job without experience, and you cannot get experience without a job! An example of this would be: Call a company that sells car opening tools and say, "I'm not a car opening expert but I would like to be one. Can I buy a set of your best car opening tools?" They will say, "No, I'm sorry; we can only sell those tools to car opening experts."

So how are you going to be a car opening expert if they will not sell you the tools? There are other types of businesses that are allowed to purchase these tools, although they are not as readily accepted into other areas like security and training. Some of them are:

- Tow Truck Drivers
- Repo Man
- Car Dealers
- Police & Firefighters
- Locksmiths & Car Opening Companies

Some suppliers do have a "We only sell to car opening companies" policy. So, to take the path of least resistance, I have written this manual with the assumption that you are going to become a car opening company.

This holds true for the other tools you will need such as lock picks, lock-picking books, and videos. All of these tools and information are considered by the car opening industry to be secrets available only to the privileged few who call themselves car openings experts. You will, of course, be buying the majority of your tools and books from suppliers who service the car opening industry. Therefore, you will need to call yourself a car opening company.

It is very difficult to get the tools you will need to run your car opening business if you are not a car opening expert. More likely than not, once you get into the car opening business you are going to have so much fun that you are probably going to want to learn how to do more of this type of work. If you are not a car opening company, we are back to the catch-22 again.

It will also be easier and cheaper to have your supplies delivered to you if you are a car opening company. According to the United States Postal Service, all car opening devices mailed within the United States are not allowed to be mailed through the Postal Service unless addressed to one of the following:

- Bona Fide Car Opening Company
- Locksmiths or Lock & Key Companies
- Bona Fide Repo Man
- Lock Manufacturer or Dealer
- Motor Vehicle Manufacturer or Dealer
- Police, Sheriff and Fire Departments

If you do not fall into one of the categories listed above, your supplies must be shipped via United Parcel Service (UPS) or Federal Express. Unfortunately UPS is more expensive and takes longer to deliver than the United States Postal Service.

One of the easiest ways to legally order your tools and have these tools in your possession is to become a car opening company. So how do you become a car opening expert? All you have to do is start your own car opening business!

You are probably thinking that this is going to be frustrating and complicated, but it's not. We are going to walk you through the five easy steps to starting your own car opening business right now! You have already completed the first step just by deciding to become a car opening business. Many people have misconceptions about the car opening industry and these misconceptions help keep the industry's image clean and give your customers a sense of trust in you. These are some of the questions that people ask me about becoming a car opening:

- Do you have to be bonded?
- Do you have to be insured?
- Do you have to be certified?
- Do you have to go to school to learn this?
- Are your fingerprints on file with police department?
- Do you need a security clearance to do this work?
- Will you to take a lie detector test to be a car opening expert?

The honest answer to all of these questions is no. If you were to ask me these questions on the street or over the phone I would answer yes to all of them and so would every other car opening expert that I know! This discourages people with police records from wanting to become car opening expert because they don't think they will pass these rigorous standards that they believe exist. It also builds an image of honor and trust in the industry.

The truth is that, at this time, the car opening industry is virtually unregulated, although every state and sometimes city or county are regulating the trade. This means there are very few cities or states that require any kind of licenses, permits, or have any other requirements to be met. With that statement said, it is your responsibility to check with your city, county and state to find out if you're regulated and what permits or licensing is required, and there is more information on this topic in “Step 2” below. This is a free market economy and anyone who wishes to become a car opening company can be one by simply hanging out a shingle. (Hanging out a shingle is a slang term for starting a business.)

This is how you start the business. First, decide what you are going to call yourself (as of today, I am a car opening).

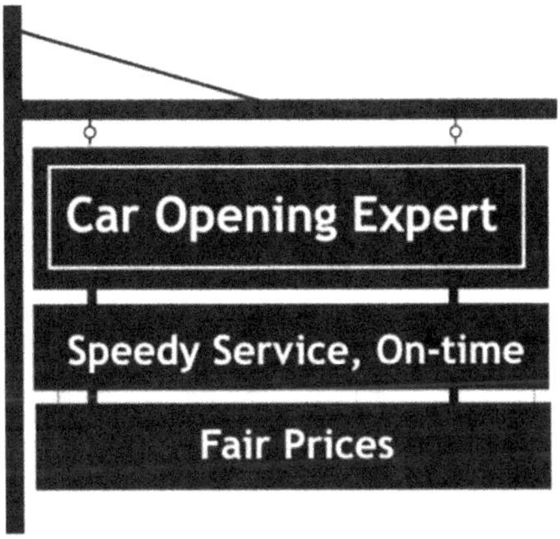

Step 2...

Is a License or Permit Is Required

The next thing you need to do is to check on whether or not the state you live in requires a license or permit to do the type of work you will be doing. Simply look online and search for the phone number of the state attorney general office. Many of these laws are on the state attorney general website. When someone answers tell them you are requesting information on the rules and regulations of operating a car opening business in your state. Many times you will get a recording requesting your name, phone number, and nature of your call. Someone will return your call. Be very patient sometimes it takes a couple of days for a representative to get back to you. If a license or permit is required, you will be notified or be told to visit the website and fill out the forms online. Be sure you print out a copy for your future record. You will receive a rules and regulations information package and you will be given the information you need to apply for any license or permit. You will also need to check with the city you live in to see if a license or permit is required to perform car opening work in that city. This is done by calling your local district attorney's office and requesting their assistance.

I'm not talking about a business license, sales tax or permit here. Right now we are checking to see if a license or permit is required to perform the type of work you will be doing. Any business that you start may require that you have a business license. When you call about rules and regulations you will be told at that time if one is required. If no one mentions it, be sure to ask! There is nothing to worry about. Everyone who applies for a business license gets one; you cannot be turned down and again online is an easy and quick way to get going.

Throughout this book we may reference the term locksmith, this is because your job opening car doors fall under this jurisdiction and you may need to follow the rules set for the locksmith industry. Fact is being known as a locksmith will open addition door when buying tools and supplies.

As of this writing there are fifteen US states that require a locksmith license;

Alabama	California
Connecticut	Illinois
Louisiana	Maryland
Nebraska	Nevada
New Jersey	New York
North Carolina	Oklahoma
Oregon	Tennessee
Texas	Virginia

More are being added every year.

Within these areas locksmiths must meet credentials established by the state they will work in. If your one of the lucky few that services these areas and is on the boarder of more than one state, you will need to find out the laws for every state you work in. Please make a note, several states license locksmith businesses separately from the individual locksmiths.

Case point: *I live in a town that requires a business license but not a locksmith license. But I* *service a small town just to the west of the city I do most of my work in. This small town requires I have a business license, tax license and a locksmith license. If I work in the town one time a year it is a ton of paperwork and fees for such a little job market. I this case I refer the business to another locksmith. He glad to get the work and I don't have the paperwork and fees.*

In some state such as Nevada, they require locksmiths to obtain a permit locally, from the sheriff of the county in which the locksmith works. However, Nevada does not establish specific criteria for who can obtain a license and the decision of whether to issue a permit is left to the sheriff.

Other Jurisdictions such as New York City and Nassau County, NY, also require locksmiths to be licensed within their jurisdiction, according to information from the Associated Locksmiths of America. Locksmiths generally must undergo a criminal background check before they are issued a license. States vary as to competency qualifications, but several states require written tests, a practical examination or both before a license can be issued.

Additional requirements may include but are not limited to these additional requirements for licensed locksmiths. Licensees may be required to prominently display their license, have an I.D. badge and check identification of the person hiring their services and keep records of all locksmith services performed for a period of several years.

Don't let this information hold you back it is not tough to get the information. It does take a small portion of time.

STEP 3...

CHOOSE A NAME FOR YOUR BUSINESS

Now it's time to choose a name for your business! Please take our advice on this subject. This, in and of itself, can be an asset or a liability to your company. Assets are good for you, liabilities are not. I have seen many companies that I believe could have been successful, but they had such silly names that people were simply afraid to call them for service.

Choosing a business name is an important step in the business planning process. Not only should you pick a name that reflects your brand identity, but you also need to ensure it is properly registered and protected for the long term. You should also give a thought to whether it's web ready and the domain name is available?

Choose your company name carefully and seriously. You are going to be in the service business and the first and possibly the only impression your customers will have of your business will be your company name. They will begin to form an opinion of your company simply from the name you've chosen. This can and will affect the number of calls you get. Your business name can make you sound like a large corporation or a small mom-and-pop operation. Your customers will never know the difference as long as you perform your service in a professional manner.

There a really simple formula that will make a name work, it's familiarity. People tend to choose service providers because they feel like they have either heard of, or seen them before. People are looking for something they can relate to.

Everyone seems to be afraid of looking foolish by making the wrong decision below is an excellent example of this.

Imagine this scene

> *I'm working on one of fifteen storefront doors. I mean fifteen doors side-by-side at a large superstore. Ninety-five percent of the people coming into and going out of the store will use the door that I'm working on! Now, are they doing this just to disturb our work and make our job take ten times as long? No! They do this because they can see that I'm working on one door and they know that it is not locked. How foolish would they look if someone saw them try to open one of the other doors and find it was locked?*

I'm trying to explain to you what I call a common obstacle to business success. A large part of your public acceptance in the service industry comes from the impression or image that a customer perceives from your business name.

This is one reason people will refer your company to others. If they know someone to recommend, they won't look foolish when someone says, "Do you know someone I can call to fix my lock?" If they have heard your name and remember it they will refer you whether they know anything about your company or not! It is for this reason that referrals are so powerful. When someone recommends a company to us, I assume that company is good or our helper would not have referred them to us. This reduces the risk of "choosing the wrong door." The referral may even be made by a stranger. I still assume the company is reputable or the stranger would not suggest you to use our services.

It is important to choose a name for your company that people can relate to. Personal names work very well such as: "YOUR first or last NAME" CAR OPENING SERVICE.

- Frank's Lockout Service
- Morris Car Opening Experts
- Casey gets you in Fast
- Emergency Road Service, by George

If your name is the same as someone they know, they assume they know you also (not actually, but the familiarity is there). It also feels more personal. Some people prefer to deal with an individual; others prefer to deal with a company. It's easy to use your own name as your business name. While there's nothing wrong with this, it does make it tougher to present a specialized image and construct professional awareness.

It really does not matter whether you choose a personal name or a company name. However, if you choose a company name, please do not try to come up with something no one has ever heard of you can use another company's name, if you like, if they are not incorporated, and if they are not in your town. Check out how many companies have the same name but are not owned by the same person. There are many because familiar names are reassuring.

- Jiffy Car Opening

- Fast Lockout Services
- Car Locks
- Expert's Lockout Co

The only problem with choosing a name that is already out there is that the first person to incorporate their business with that name owns that name for the entire state. As soon as one person owns a name they can make everyone else with the same name stop using it (if they want to). Choosing a name that people are already familiar with will put you way ahead of the competition. It doesn't have to be an exact copy of a name; something that sounds like something else will do.

How will your name look on letterheads and logos and will it be good for the internet, as part of a shirt emblem or label, on social media.

What implications does it evoke, is your name too corporate or not corporate enough or does it reflect your business viewpoint and philosophy? Does it appeal to the emergency needs of your customer?

Is it distinctive enough not to interfere with other local competitors? Choose a name that does not sound or look like it is someone else's and may have not been claimed by somebody in your city or county, online or offline. A quick web search and domain name search will alert you to any current use.

Pick a name that can be web ready or easily modified in order to claim a website address; your business name needs to be unique and available. But keep it short, the customer needs to remember you and how to spell the name if they search for you. When using the info on a website, the subtext under your name should also be rich in key words that reflect what your business does. To see if you're on the right track do find out if your business name has been claimed online, do a simple web search to see if anyone is already using that name. Modify it a bit if it's being used and try again. Here's a few ideas; Speedy, Quick, Simple, Zippy's, On-Time, Prompt, Early, Flash are just a few.

Next, check whether a domain name (or web address) is available. You can do this using the WHOIS database of domain names. If it is available, be sure to claim it right away.

Claim your social media identity very quickly; in today's market this is extremely important. It's a good idea to claim your social media name early in the naming process, even if you are not sure which sites you intend to use. A name for your Facebook page can be set up and changed, but you can only claim a vanity name or custom name once you've got 25 fans or "likes." This custom name must be unique and unclaimed.

Register your business name is a confusing area for new business owners. It encompasses a procedure known as recording a "Doing Business As" (DBA) name or trade name. This process shouldn't be confused with incorporation and it doesn't provide trademark protection. Registering your "Doing Business As" name is simply the process of letting your state government know that you are doing business as a name other than your personal name or the. Quick note: If you are operating under your own name, then you can skip the process.

If you decide you want to use a trademark then getting it protected may be a viable step for you. A trademark protects words, names, symbols, and logos that distinguish goods and services. Your name is one of your most valuable business assets, so it's worth protecting. You can file for a trademark for less than $300.

If people hear your company name and think, "Oh yes, I've heard of your company," you've got a winner!

STEP 4...
REGISTER TRADE NAME/TAX LICENSE

Now that you have chosen a name for your business the next thing to do is to make sure that no one else in your town is using that business name. We'll refer to the name you've chosen as your "Trade Name" which will also be known as your "DBA." This is short for "Doing Business As" and is the proper terminology for the name you've chosen to do business under.

Trade Name - noun. Is name of a business or one of its products which, by use of the name and public reputation, identifies the product as that of a business. A trade name belongs to the first business to use it, and the identification and reputation give it value and the right to protect the trade name against its use by others.

DBA stands for "Doing Business As," which is a company name, also commonly called a "fictitious business name", "trade name" or "assumed name". A DBA is a secondary name for your business, an officially licensed "alias" if you will. When a sole proprietor operates a company using any name except his or her own given name, then the DBA or fictitious business name registration establishes the legal ownership to satisfy banks, local authorities, customers, etc.

The way you find out if the name you've chosen is available for you to use or if it is already being used by someone else, is to have a trade name search done. A trade name search is done at no charge and while you wait at the Department of Revenue in your town. It can also be done online; many are free as well as the paid services. I recommend starting with the "Free" sites and do this for the state you wish to start the business in. If the trade name search comes up clear and no one else is using that name in your trade classification (you'll be able to see if someone else is using that name but not in your trade classification, you can still use it), be sure you double check the name with a different source, at this point you can register your trade name. Examples of "same name, different classification" are:

- City Expert Car Opening Service
- Quick Car Opening Service
- Fastest Car Opening in Town

You can see above the names are different, yet the idea of your core name "Car Opening" is reflected with each of these different names.

Once you find a name that you can use, you will need to register your trade name with the Department of Revenue so that no one else can use it. You can register your trade name at the same office and normally with the same person who has done your search for you. It's just a matter of filling out a form and paying a small fee. Your Trade Name Registration confirmation letter from the Department of Revenue, so places will hand you your confirmation letter at the same time you make your payment, yet other county's will arrive by mail in about two weeks. You will need to take this letter with you when you open your business checking account. You will have to open a business checking account in order to be able to deposit checks, use your phone based credit card processing, cash money orders that are made out to your company name.

Most of the information to find your trade name can be done online at:

> *Search Business Licenses — this is done on your states government website. If your search result is "No matches were found for your search," try spelling the name differently or leave out abbreviations or punctuation such as Inc, LLC, etc.*
>
> *"Your" State Department of Revenue — this online database search is intended for use by the general public as a consumer protection program, and includes some trade names.*
>
> *"Your" Secretary of State Corporations Registration Data Search — Corporation and limited liability company names.*
>
> *Patent and Trademark Commission — Search for federally registered names at this website, http://www.uspto.gov.*

Who Needs A Sales Tax License? Who is required to have a sales tax license? - Individuals or businesses that sell tangible personal property to the final consumer need a sales tax license. An application for a sales tax license may be obtained on your city, county and state websites. Each state has their own tax code and your job as a business owner will be to know the laws of your city, county, state and of course the national laws on your business. All of this information is online as well as at your local and county government offices.

You are providing a service (considered labor), and while you are at the Department of Revenue you need to check to see if your city or state requires you to charge taxes on labor. If it does, you will also need to apply for a tax license. Actually you may need two of these, one for the city and one for the state. You can get the state license at the Department of Revenue while you are there. You'll have to go downtown to the city offices to get the city tax license.

I suggest that you go ahead and get both of these tax licenses anyway (city and state). If you decide you want to sell products at some time in the future (and by the way, you can sell products that have nothing to do with the business you are in), with these licenses you will be able to do so. Also, when you buy these products for resale, you will not have to pay taxes on them yourself.

Below is an example of one states sales tax laws;

> *City/Local/County Sales Tax – "Your State" has no city, local, or county sales tax. The state sales tax rate is 6%.*
>
> *Retailers - Retailers make sales to the final consumer. Sales tax of 6% on their retail sales must be remitted to the State of "Your State". In addition, retailers must be licensed to collect tax from their customers and remit the sales tax to the State of "Your State".*

<u>Wholesalers</u> - Wholesalers sell to other wholesalers or retailers and not to the final consumer. The price at which the seller sells a product does not determine if the seller is a wholesaler. The determination is based on whom the products are sold to by the seller. Wholesalers buy for resale at wholesale. They are not making retail sales; therefore registration for sales tax is not required. Wholesalers claiming an exemption should provide a written statement that they are purchasing for "resale at wholesale".

<u>Contractors</u> - A sales tax license is not required for contractors or subcontractors, since they are the final consumers of the materials they affix to real property. Anyone who is directly engaged in the activity of constructing, altering, repairing, or improving real estate for others is liable for the sales tax on the inventory value of the materials affixed to the property. If the real estate being constructed, altered, repaired, or improved is a nonprofit hospital or nonprofit housing entity, no tax is due on any materials which became affixed to and made a structural part of the hospital or housing entity. This information may be obtained in Revenue Administrative Bulletin 1988-35 and 1999-02.

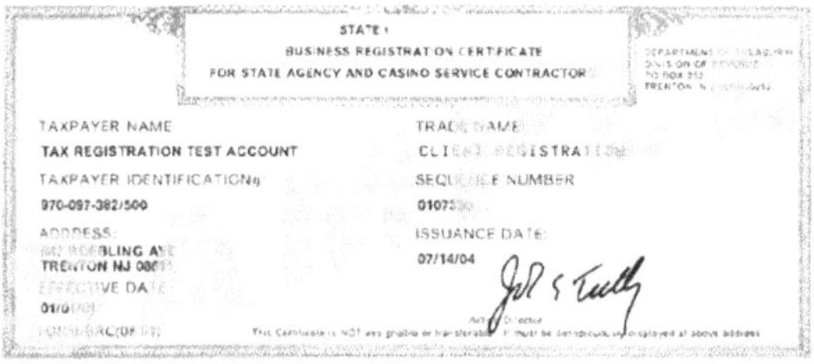
BUSINESS REGISTRATION CERTIFICATE
FOR STATE AGENCY AND CASINO SERVICE CONTRACTOR

TAXPAYER NAME
TAX REGISTRATION TEST ACCOUNT

TAXPAYER IDENTIFICATION#
970-097-382/500

ADDRESS:
TRENTON NJ

SEQUENCE NUMBER

ISSUANCE DATE:
07/14/04

<u>Services</u> - Businesses repair, improve, or alter tangible personal property owned by others. Businesses, who sell tangible personal property in

addition to providing labor or a service, are required to obtain a sales tax license. Any property which goes with the customer in connection with the repair or service is considered a sale at retail and subject to sales tax.

Out-of-State Businesses - For transactions occurring on or after October 1, 2015, an out-of-state seller may be required to remit sales or use tax on sales into "Your State". See Notice of New Sales and Use Tax Requirements for Out-of-State Sellers.

Remember that the above is an example and you will need to gather the required information for your state, county and city. It is your responsibility to follow the laws of your jurisdiction.

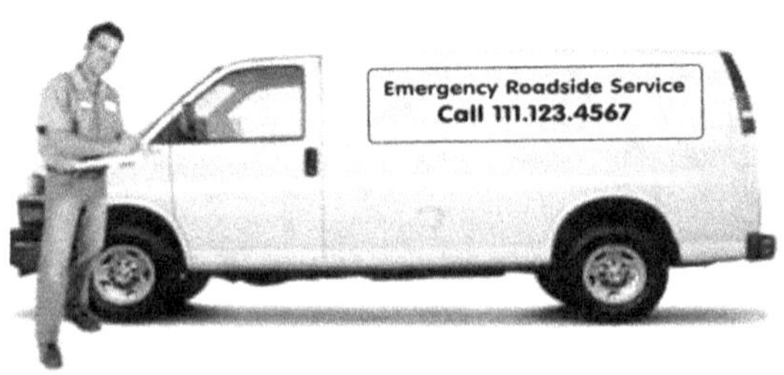

STEP 5...

BUSINESS CARD, ENVELOPE, STATIONERY

The next thing you need to do is get some business cards printed. This will be the most important tool in your possession. You will need to become a professional business card dispensing machine!

> ***Read Section on Advertising*** *for tips and tricks on how to design your business cards. Remember, this is your most important tool and I have suggestions that will make this tool very powerful!*
>
> ***Read Section on Communications*** *because you will need to choose a phone number to print on your cards. Knowing how you want to handle your incoming calls should be decided at this time.*
>
> ***Read Section on Insurance*** *to decide if you wish to be bonded and insured and if this is something you would like to advertise on your cards.*

With most business being done digitally, you might think that business cards don't matter anymore. But they can offer a lot. Here's why they're still important for business and how you can get the most out of yours.

Business cards still matter because our memory sucks. How many times have you met someone, spent most of the conversation thinking of what to say so you don't sound stupid, and then promptly forget their name when it's all over?

What do you do? You introduce yourself and describe what you do, but at some point, you'll need to hand off your contact information. A business card saves you time and makes you look professional. You're not fumbling around with a pen to scribble your email address on a cocktail napkin, and you also give them a sense that this isn't your first rodeo.

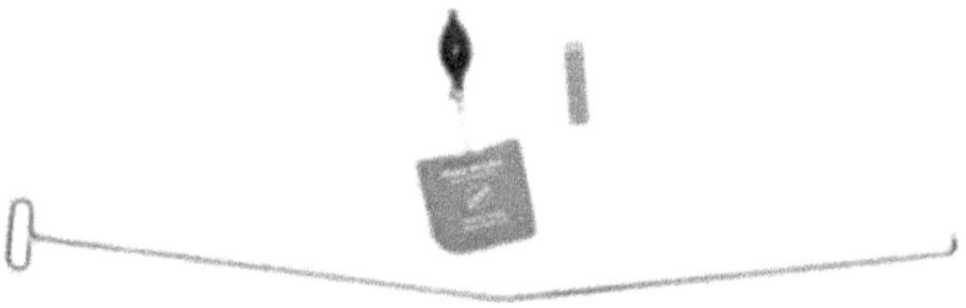

Here are a few thoughts of what your business card can do for you:

- *Tell people your name and the name of your business.*
- *Provide prospects with a way to contact you.*
- *Give others a taste of your work, style and personality.*
- *It can be so unusual or attractive or strange or charming or funny that it sticks in the memory like a great radio or television ad.*
- *It can be reused, as it passes from person to person, giving the same message to each person who comes in contact with it.*

The two main functions of your card are to gain business from the person you give it to and to get your name out to other people with whom the first person comes in contact with via referrals.

Get started, have them made locally or on line and at the same time you are having your cards printed you should have envelopes printed with your business name and address in the return address area. You will also need a letterhead with your business name and address printed at the top of the page. A letterhead is simply a blank 8.5"x11" sheet of paper with your business name and address printed on it. You will use it to write letters to suppliers and customers. Many companies will not open an account for you if you do not write your request for credit on your company letterhead.

Don't spend a lot of time trying to lay out designs for your cards, envelopes, and letterhead. Just go right down to a print shop and tell them what you want according to the guidelines I've given you. They have all kinds of ready-made artwork that you can use and will sit down with you and help you design these things. If you try to do it yourself you're going to knock yourself out, and before long you won't know if you like what you've come up with or not! The people at the print shop can show you how things will look on a computer before you agree to have it done. The whole process can take less than an hour!

CONGRATULATIONS! If you have completed the first five steps, by the power vested in your state with the issuance of tax licenses and trade name registration (and operating licenses or permits if required), you are now officially a car opening. The documents you now possess are considered proof thereof.

Note: Your cards, envelopes, and letterhead are sometimes all the proof required by suppliers and are normally only necessary with your first order. It is not necessary, nor is it recommended, that you tell anyone that you have no experience at all. A good answer when someone asks you how long you have been doing this is, “Oh, for a while now.” Now that you have become a car opening you can order your tools and begin your training.

Sample Business Card

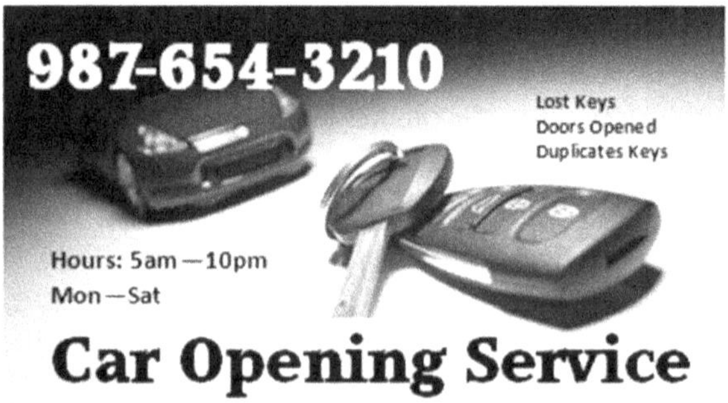

Sample Business Card

STEP 6...

ORDER TOOLS, BOOKS AND YOUTUBE

Skip ahead to Chapter Twelve, this is the chapter on where to purchase your tools and what type of tools will be needed and what cost are involved. Get these tools coming, many of the places can you order from can get them to you with "Next Day Service" Once you placed the order come back to this page and continue your journey.

Welcome back... At this point you should have ordered your tools. Thoroughly examine and study your tools and any books once they have arrived.

In the meantime watch some YouTube.com it is one of the easiest places to get a basic knowledge on how to use your tools, just remember that not everything on this site is real. The best way to learn is "Hands On" and there is no better way to learn then doing the actual work. Learning the hard way, through experience is far more valuable then reading or watching videos. Knowledge through YouTube is extremely valuable, but may not be as accurate in all cases.

After you have studied these you will need some "Hands On" experience and practice. Start with your own car, then your wife's car and continue until you find the job becoming easier. Use the first recommended kit in Chapter Twelve (SKU: AK42-Mega). Do try some of the tricks on YouTube many are not as easy as they show you. Be sure to try different makes and models as well as different years of manufacturing.

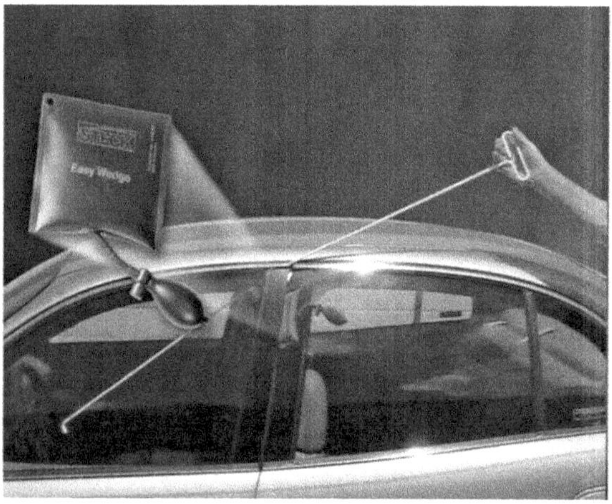

Below is kit (SKU: AK42-Mega).

STEP 7...

DEVELOP YOUR SKILLS AND PRACTICE

There are a few more things I need to do before I get my first paying customer! The next two things I need to do are to learn about the paperwork that I will need to run this business and how to charge and collect our fees. Once again jump ahead and read the section on "Paperwork" will show which kinds of invoices to use and other forms associated with this business.

The section on Money Matters discusses how to charge for your services and the different methods of payment you may wish to accept.

The below price list is "NOT" updated and are examples only, they are for information only.

It not very professional to fly by the seat of your pants and is important to have a set price sheet. This price sheet can change at any time… it's your business.

Price List

We offer a $19 Service call fee in order to cover travel expenses for mobile on-site service.

Lock Change	Starting at $25 *
Lock Rekey	Starting at $19 *
Car Lockout	Starting at $25 *
House Lockout	Starting at $25 *
Car Key / Ignition Replacement	Starting at $90 *
Transponder Car Key / Ignition Replacement	Starting at $119 *
Safe Lockout	Starting at $45 *
Mail Box / File Cabinet Lockout	Starting at $35 *
Mail Box / File Cabinet Change	Starting at $25 *
Fresh Lock Installation	Starting at $45 *
Car Key Extraction	Starting at $75 *

* Price quotes are a minimum. Every service has it's unique complications... Further inspection is needed, call now so our professional can arrive as soon as possible.

Important Note: Unforseen complications may arise at the site, these changes may affect the price by way of labor or parts. In any circumstance, changes to the final price will be explained before any work is done.

Sample of a price List

STEP 8...

DEVELOP A CUSTOMER BASE

Let's make sure you look the part by reading the section on Appearances. If you have your invoices printed you are ready for customers. Wait, remember, if you are going to have checks made out to anything other than your personal name you will have to have a business checking account open in your business name to deposit and/or cash those checks.

You need to be prepared for any problems that you might encounter so let's read the section on Problems and then go right into the section on Getting Business. Now you can start handing out those business cards and building our business!

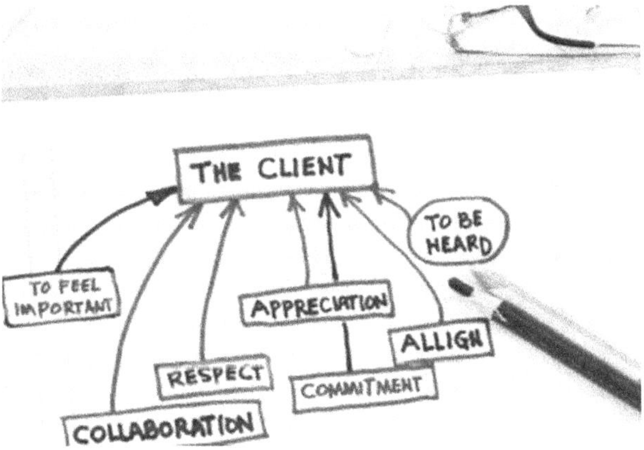

It's important to develop a customer base.

STEP 9...

HAVE FUN AND MAKE MONEY

This has just been too easy. The next section to read win be Telephone Skills and this is very important. Practice your telephone skills and always ask yourself after every phone call that ended without a sale, "How could I have spoken to that customer differently that would have made them decide to use my service?" This will take some time. Have your friends call you pretending to be customers. This will help you feel more self-assured when you begin talking with real customers.

The remaining sections of the manual can be read at your leisure. Your business should be up and running by this time. The section on The Law is general information. If you received a rules and regulation package from your city or state, it will have more specific laws that relate to your area.

Take the time to read the sections on Trade Associations and continuing your education. We recommend that you join one of the national associations, or join a local group in your town.

I've have also included a list of Suppliers to give you many sources to order your tools and supplies from. Sometimes just finding these contacts is the hardest part of starting a business.

STEP 10...

TALK TO A BOOKKEEPER OR ACCOUNTANT

As soon as you start earning and collecting money, you will need to seek out professional help to keep you from getting into trouble with the Internal Revenue Service. A competent bookkeeper or accountant should be found. These professionals should know the rules of business and can answer any paperwork related questions you may have about your business.

This business is very simple, the rules are also simple, but you need to know what the rules are for your city and state. The IRS says, "Ignorance is no excuse."

WARNING: The IRS will not let you off the hook just because you were not aware of the rules!

CHAPTER TWO

ADVERTISING

The purpose of advertising boils down to just one thing, getting more business and doing more jobs. The better your advertising is, the more profit you will make. If you're promotions are correctly targeted into the market which you have an interest in or you feel as a large customer base, the more profit you will make. Another factor to consider is the number of prospective customers you will reach and how you are advertising is presented to them. There are many things that you will do in your business, and advertising will play the big important role in getting new business and referrals.

Advertising is a must

You've seen or heard catchy ads on the radio, TV, even bus stop bench advertising and seen good business cards. You probably even have some type of advertising in your possession right now. Stop a minute and think... Then look into your wallet or purse and see what forms of advertising that you have kept. Now ask yourself why do I still have this in my possession and do I want this for some particular reason? Here are a few thoughts, maybe you need the service or you're saving a discount coupon. Keep in mind that this is what advertising is all about and this is what you're trying to achieve. It's about getting your prospective customer to remember you and why you are better than your competitor.

Advertise Skillfully

In the car opening business you will not meet anyone who has not needed your services in the past or who might need you to open his car door sometime in the future. Just mentioning that you are a car opening expert is a form of advertising.

There are many ways to advertise and just as many ways to pay someone else to do this for you. Your own effort will pay for itself many times over. Word of mouth is by far the best advertising that you will ever have. Let's not forget social media, blogs, YouTube and mobile websites, these areas reach a multitude of people that never see paper ads. You want your prospective customers remember your company name or phone number when they are in a frenzy to get the keys in their car? Your willingness to have different types of advertising is as good as your imagination.

It is important in this business that you do not use cute, clever, or funny advertising. This will be a handicap to any advertising that you do. You need to remember that this is a unique business. Silly advertising does not look "professional" and it does not reassure your customers that you are a professional. They want the business that can be on-time, looks professional, and can get them in their car in a fast and polite manner. Your advertising should show, tell and promote this professionalism.

Keep your advertising professional.

They won't remember how fast you are, but they will remember how well they had been treated.

Business Cards

Your business cards will sometimes be the first impression that your new customer will receive about your company. The best cards that I've have seen are the ones that convey a little extra information, like your slogan or your company message. In designing your business cards there are several things to keep in mind. Limited space, vital information, visual recognition, and a reason for keeping the card are important. Since your business card is so small, the impact of your card is very important. Impact can be many things: color, size of print, or the layout of the graphics.

Your card needs to have a reason why they should keep your card and not your competitor. Here is a few thought on why someone would keep your card.

or

Spend a few extra dollar to look professional.

Here are the top 5 reasons **WHY** people keep *business cards.*

Make money *- In most cases, you're offering something that will save time, increase productivity and efficiency, and ultimately result in additional or saved revenue. Make sure your business card lets prospects know that you can help them make more money.*

Save money *- Coupons, discounts and other promotions are a great way to keep business cards. Make sure your offer is contingent on presenting your business card to redeem the savings. This technique is often employed by retailers and personal service companies such as your car opening service.*

Earn rewards *- You could turn the back of your business card into a punch sheet that's stamped every time a customer uses your services. Once all the punches are filled, they'll get a free service. Your business can benefit from the repeat business with this type of business card it can generate revenue and if the reward is good enough, you can almost guarantee that your card won't be thrown away or forgotten.*

Useful information *- Adding useful information such as sports schedules, event calendars and conversion charts are a great way to keep your business cards in the wallets, purses and rolodexes of your prospects and customers. Work hard at understanding your target market and give them something they'll use and keep.*

Because it looks great *- The easiest way to get your card tossed into the recycle bin is to look unprofessional; conversely, one of the* *best ways to keep it in the hands of prospects is to make sure your business card looks professional.*

Make sure you have a professionally designed business card, and have it professionally printed. You can try to get creative by having your card die cut with sleek rounded corners or other shapes. Regardless of anything else you do, if your business card looks bad your company will look bad. If your business card looks great, then you'll look great and all your other business card elements will help seal the deal.

Business Card Information

Your company's name, address, city, state, zip and important, REMEMBER your phone number should "**standout**". It is important that your business card have most if not all the following information that is listed below. The key to using business cards is getting your customers to keep them, here are a few thoughts.

- Business Name
- **Phone Number**
- Type of business *(lockout specialist, alarms, general car opening, etc.)*
- Business hours or location if you have a shop
- Slogan, message or reason why your customers should keep your card. Some other ideas might be: bonded, insured, certified or mobile only
- If run your business on a part-time basis simply state on your card what your hours are.

For example:

- *6 pm through 6 am, Mon/Fri*
- *24 hr. / 7 days*
- *Sat & Sun only*
- *Closed on Sunday's*

Discount Coupon

If you are willing to make your card a discount coupon for, let's say, 10% off each time your card is presented, people will be much more inclined to keep it. This is also a good source for referrals. Someone holding your card may have the opportunity to help a friend or stranger by giving them your discount card. It gives them a chance to be helpful and it makes people feel good.

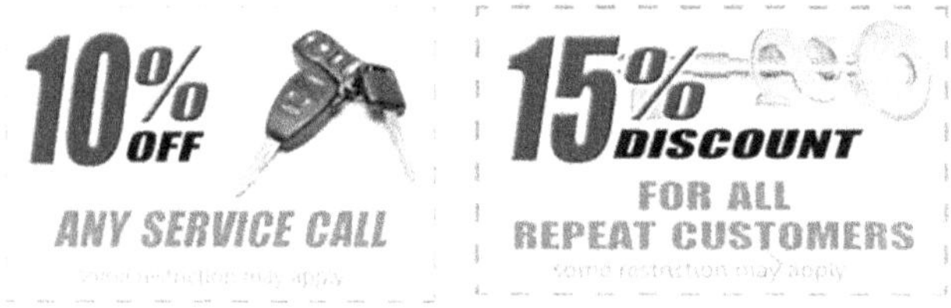

Add a touch of color to your ads.

Visual recognition

When your customer sees your card they instantly remember you or your business. This can be from seeing a picture, logo or graphic of what you do or type your service you give, just keep it simple, the simpler the better.

Colored cards / Photo Cards

When printed effectively, colored cards are very striking and will give your company the appearance of being successful.

Who should you give your business cards to? Everyone you meet, plus many more. Each time you hand out your card, hand out three cards. Ask your prospective customer to give two of them away. You will be surprised at the number of people who will do this for you. If you give several business cards away several times a day, within a short period of time the phone will start ringing so much that there won't be enough time to do all the work.

Of all the information on your card, the **phone number** should stand out the most. If people can't read it or the print is too small, they probably will not keep your card. Keeping this in mind, you still need to give them a reason to keep your card. One good way is to give them something for free. This could be a small gift such as a key chain or a discount for using your service.

Magnetic cards

These magnetic cards are very valuable when used correctly. You will give these to store clerks and used car dealers, hotel clerks, and anyone who will display your card for quick reference. Store clerks will place this on the cash registers to help customers, and used car dealers will want this close by for emergencies.

Rolodex cards

These cards are the ones that fit into a card file. This is your basic business card only larger and it is an excellent item to stuff into your statements when you are mailing them. Give these to customers that you are meeting for the first time and your old customers that you have had for a long time. When you print these cards with all of your important information, your customer does not have to do a thing except file the card. This is a genuine benefit to them, which makes it a genuine benefit for you.

You would think that this is a thing of the past, but it's not. Stop and think about how many times a person in a parking lot locks there keys in their car, then goes to a nearby business and asked for help. The owner reaches under the counter and pulls out his Rolodex. These are the people you should be giving both a business card too as well as a Rolodex card.

Websites (phone enabled)

In today's day and age the need for a website a must and there is normally a monthly fee associated with it, but the price is minimal. One of the companies that I recommend is called WIX (www.wix.com) they are very basic and most people can work their way through the process to get a web page up and running.

What needs to be on your website: The same basic things that are on your business card plus a little more. You could elaborate on your services, tell your customers how fast your service is, and give your hours of business. Tell them if you do emergency work, if you have 24-hour service, what areas you cover, and maybe even tell what types of payment that you will accept. Plus be visual, people want to see your services, that's the point of a website, to "See your product or service."

Why the website advertising: Ever since the smart phones started becoming more popular everyone is using them as their first place to look when getting the help they need. I still have the yellow pages under my desk but when I want to find someone for help I go to my computer and jump on the internet to find what I need. When I am out on a jobsite I will use my smart phone every time... no fail.

Mobile Phones Website

To even be more up to date and to have a jump on today's market place, a mobile phone website with a few built in features such as "Push to Dial" will pay for itself in a very short period of time. With most people having smart phones, the uses of paper phone book ads are going by the way of the dinosaur. The WIX website company also has the technology to turn your website into a mobile website, with almost no effort on your part. They use your webpage info and will create a mobile website from it. If you think this is not your cup of tea, stop and think of a few things that are long gone, such as; pay phone that uses coins, glass soda bottles, folding tape measure (that's a real old one) and this is just a few items. Think further into the future and stay ahead of the advertising curve. This is where the money is to be made, not in the comfortable past.

Mobile Phone website are the future, every man women and most children have a smart phone today.

SOCIAL MEDIA

Social media itself is a catch-all term for sites that may provide radically different social actions. For instance, Twitter is a social site designed to let people share short messages or "updates" with others. Facebook, in contrast is a full-blown social networking site that allows for sharing updates, photos, joining events and a variety of other activities.

Social media marketing (SMM) is a form of Internet marketing that utilizes social networking websites as a marketing tool. The goal of SMM is to produce content that users will share with their social network to help a company increase brand exposure and broaden customer reach.

This is a list short of the more active social media sites; Facebook, Instagram, Twitter, Pinterest, Google+, LinkedIn, YouTube. There are many more and new ones come and go every day, watch the trends and participate in the areas you feel comfortable in.

What are the potential problems?

When using social media, you should bear in mind that, though the sites are generally free to use, you will need to make an investment of time. Plus informal, off-the-cuff remarks can and will appear unprofessional and could harm your reputation and obvious ‘selling’ can be a turn-off for users.

You will also need to be sure that you’re engaging with the right people, and that your efforts are bringing some reward. Social media marketing may be just that "social" but its successful use by small businesses is far from casual.

Yellow Pages Advertising

This form of advertising medium is disappearing fast, yet many old shops still think they need it. I am no longer in this mind set; with that in mind I still carry a phone book in my van. It’s not the small quality of information anymore and I have found my smart phone is far more valuable than this old outdated system. It is mainly used to verify addresses of customers or when I write some information down incorrect. But I do not have any of this style advertising unless it was free. The monthly rates are very expensive if they make a mistake in your ad it will be one year before it is corrected. I would invest in a website that is phone enabled (smart phone can find and it looks good on all the different types and styles of phones.)

Specialty Numbers

Some car opening companies use pretty catchy phone numbers that are easy to remember such as: 555-OPEN or 555-LOCK. If you can come up with one of these it would be beneficial and would help people remember your number, but this is not a critical factor to your business success. Ask your phone company representative for information on these types of numbers. Plus there is an up-charge to your phone bill for these types of phone numbers.

There is one issue that I have with these types of phone numbers. It is the ability to have your customers remember it and the number not being confusing. This may sound obvious but I know of a competitor that his specialty number is confusing. This is an example: If your number was 345-3456, seems easy, but I know for a fact that I spend more time repeating this number back to the customer. This is because they think you stated it wrong or they heard the number wrong. This problem is from repeating the same three numbers twice. Just be careful when picking your number.

Flyers and Direct Mail

This form of advertising is inexpensive and can be very profitable if you direct it to a target market or groups of customers that use car opening services. This form of advertisement can be tailored to fit a group, area or the type of customer that you would like to do business with. Be sure that you get professional help on the art work and keep things as simple as you can.

Keep in mind these basic rules and ideas when doing your direct mail flyers. Send to a predetermined and targeted group of clients. Be sure these people meet the criteria of your objective. Here is a few thoughts on who might use your services; used car dealer, small businesses or real estate offices, fast food chains, strip malls, etc. All of these can be very profitable. Customize your mailer to fit your customers' needs. Don't try to sell them lockout services if they really need a tow truck service. Be sure to speak directly to them in your mailer and fill "their" need not yours. Design with the purpose of getting them to remember your name, hang the flyer up or file it for future reference. This could be done with a slogan, some eye-catching logos and graphics, or printing your phone number big and bold along with your company name. Sending out this advertising need repetition, one time is not enough, you will need to do this several time but the results will start to show almost immediately.

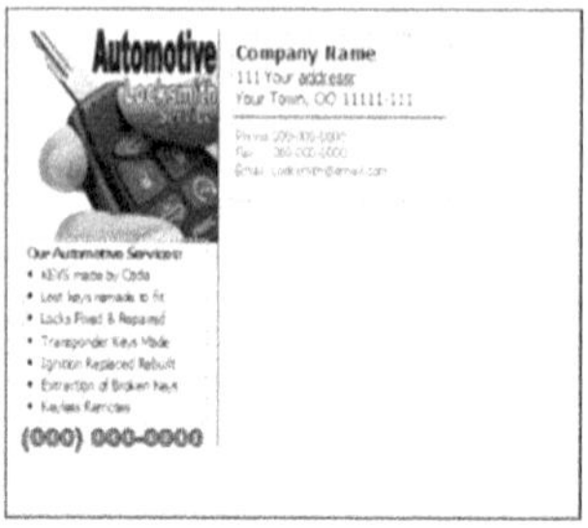

The side of the card everyone looks at is the side with their name on it... Use it!

The basic reasons you should use flyers are that the cost per each piece you send out is relatively small and that you can target a very narrow clientele. By this I mean you, as a car opening expert, can pick the type of businesses that you think will be most beneficial to you. Your flyer can be customized to fit the needs of car rental agencies one time, and then do a flyer just for your fast food places, and even emergency road service companies. Your flyers need to fit the customers who you wish to do business with, yes a generic flyer will work, just not as well as a tailored one.

The flow of your flyer should be from some type of graphic that represents what you do and the words tells your story, the fewer the words the better. You are trying to communicate to your potential customer what your company does without them working very hard to figure it out, the easier the better. Remember most people scan your document, they do not read it. So catch the eye with a memorable easy to “scan and remember” flyer.

The graphics should be simple but very clear. Be sure the graphics make a point that you’re giving them a professional service and making a looking flyer always helps. Good graphics will also make clear what you are trying to sell them. This "sell is for your service and/or products that you provide. Color is not as important but does help draw more attention to specific areas in the flyer. Be very specific about the topics that you choose. One last idea, the always look for their name and that area is the most valuable portion of you flyer, use it very wisely.

Newspapers and Free Advertising

Newspapers are another form of name recognition advertising but will not cause immediate measurable increases in your business. News releases are a form of free advertising. The hard part is finding something new and interesting that the newspapers want to print. Just because you think that you have the newest and best widget does not mean that the editor of the newspaper will think it is great. Smaller newspapers will be your best bet when it comes to news releases as long as your story is not presented as self-benefiting. A story about the costs of breaking a window versus paying someone to open your car could be a great news release story.

Signs on Your Vehicle

This area of advertising is a must. You should have signs on your vehicle as well as on your place of business if you have a shop. Don't be cheap when it comes to your business image. A ratty looking sign will reflect poorly on your business. Of all the advertising that you do, this is one place where you should spend the extra money to get a professional job done. Let the quality of your sign reflect the quality of work that you do. Be original and use your logo, and be sure to tie all this in with the theme of your business.

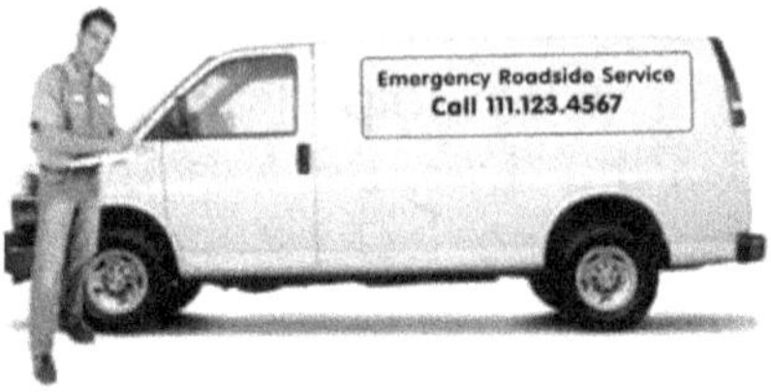

Use your moving bill board to advertise.

Radio and Television

Television is not recommended when starting out because of the expense. TV gets about the same results as radio: good for name recognition, not for immediate sales. Start in areas where you can measure immediate increases in your business and then work on name recognition.

Radio follows listeners everywhere in the home and on the highway. It's known for lower rates compared with other types of advertising. In the field of car opening, it may be good for recognition but won't do a lot for emergency lockout services. If you are trying to have your customers recognize your name when they need you in the future, this is a good way to start.

In general terms radio and television advertising should be and are that is used after you have become well established. It's good for long term results and not for the entrepreneur starting out.

Advertising Referrals

Referrals are one of the best forms of advertising that you will "never" pay for. This form of advertising is done by your good will and from quality work that you perform. If you can get one referral from each customer you help, you will never need any other form of advertising.

Networking

Make valuable contacts by joining local trade associations or professional organizations. By joining groups such as your local chamber of commerce, you'll get to rub shoulders with other small business owners like you and develop some potentially fruitful relationships. Even if the business owners you meet may not need your services, they may pass your name on to others if you make a favorable impression. Getting involved with your church or local charities is another good way to generate referrals.

Asking

You can generate a large number of referrals simply by asking for them. The best time to ask is usually just after completing a transaction where the customer is highly satisfied with your work. If you're a life insurance agent, for example, and your new policyholder is happy with your caring and professional approach, ask if he knows of any friends or family members who could also benefit from your services. In some cases, a satisfied customer may even make the contact for you.

CHAPTER THREE

COMMUNICATIONS

Communications is a very important area that needs to be addressed. There are many ways that you can set up your communication system. If you do not do it properly you could be cutting your business in half. I've see this being done wrong every day and all I can say is… more for us!

Your telephone system is simply the way in which you handle your incoming calls. In this section I will tell you exactly how to handle your incoming calls for optimum performance, which equates to getting as many jobs as possible. There are many communication devices available to choose from such as business telephones, residential telephones, cellular phones, answering services, radios, and voicemail.

CELLULAR PHONES

Clearly, the best way to handle incoming calls is to personally answer each and every call yourself. This will ensure that the business line is always answered in a professional manner. The phone line that you are going to use for your business needs to have call waiting, call forwarding and voice mail activated. These features are standard on most cellphones if they are not it would be wise to get them.

This is the standard voicemail message that I use for our customers. I've found this message to be better than anything else I've tried in order to get someone to leave a message...

> *"Hello, you have reached 'your business name.' We are being alerted to your call. Please leave a message and we will return your call as soon as possible. Thank you."*

"We are being alerted to your call" gives the impression that I will call them back immediately, and I have found this phrase to be the most successful in getting a potential customer to leave a message.

Try to answer every call, if not have a quality message that will attract more business.

When setting up the voicemail speak clearly and what we are talking about is recording the message in a quiet undisturbed place. Speak in a manner that both young people as well as the older generation will understand what you are trying to communicate.

Give as much information as you can without the voicemail becoming too long and boring, the idea is to have them leave info so you can call them back in a reasonable time. Again, short but informative is the goal.

Answering Services

Answering services have a place in your business and are mainly used when you need some time off. They have some good points and some bad points. Of course, the obvious good point is that you actually have a physical person answering the phone. Unfortunately, this real person doesn't know what your prices are or how soon you can respond. You will lose business if you are answering all of your calls through an answering service. People do not want to wait to find out if you can come help them out.

One of the good things about an answering service is, at night when you stop working, your business will continue to have a person answering the phone and taking messages with a real people, not voicemail. This works very well if you want to stop at 6:00 p.m. so that you can go do some of those extracurricular activities. Just call forward your phones to the answering service. The service will take messages so you won't physically have to answer the phone. It is always good to have a person answering the phone, but you do not have to accept every job that comes in.

Caller ID

You are probably already familiar with Caller ID. You will want to have this service so you will know when your competition is price checking you or its regular customer in which you feel need to be a priority call when two calls come in at the same time. The only drawback is anyone who does not want you to know who is calling can block their number by dialing two extra numbers before they call you. Almost all smart phones have this as a built in feature once you program your customers name to the number. Just remember that your customers may have more phone numbers than just one. If their number has not has been preprogramed into your phone you will not have a clue who is calling you.

One thought on area codes. If you live in a town that has a military base the area code could be coming from anywhere in the country and still be local person wanting you to unlock there vehicle.

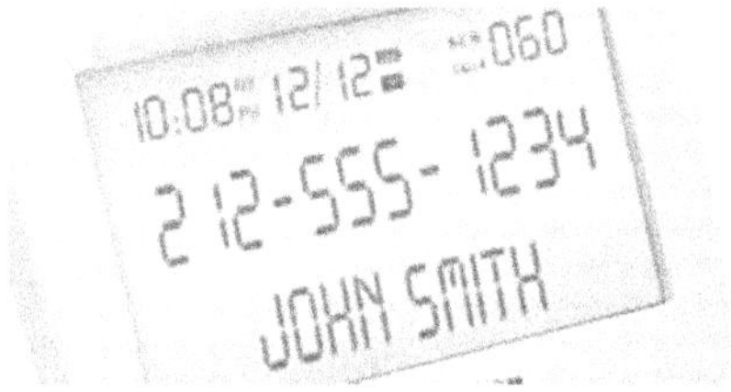

CHAPTER FOUR

INSURANCE

In this section I will give you a basic idea of the different kinds of insurance that are associated with the car opening business. Your best resources to find out state requirements; cost associated with business and coverage is through your local insurance agent. I don't claim to be insurance agent. So, whatever you do, always consider talking to an insurance professional about your needs.

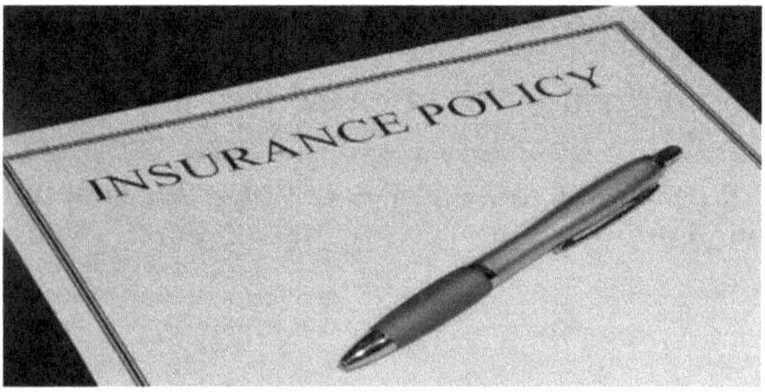

Everyone dislikes insurance, until it's needed.

Every state has different requirements and insurance is very important. Some states require that you carry certain types of insurance. Other states don't require any form of insurance. You should carry the insurance that you need to protect yourself, your van, your business, and your family. Yes, insurance is a big consideration when just starting out. Remember it is a minor expense if something goes wrong and being over protected is not always a negative when you need it.

Insurance agents are more than willing to give you estimates on cost of these policies. They are salespeople that earn a living from writing policies to the small business people. There are two basic types of agents; independent agents that sell policies from more than one insurer and exclusive agents work for only one insurance company. Just in case your insurance person does not have all the types of policies that you need, you may ask an independent agent. Some of the sales people will come to your place of business or even your home to make a sale.

AUTOMOTIVE

This is by far the most common type of insurance. Most types of this coverage have several parts that I will cover.

COLLISION COVERAGE

Insurance designed to pay for the repair or replacement of the policy owner's car in the event of an accident, no matter who caused the accident. Collision coverage usually requires the payment of a deductible when a claim is made and may be required to secure a new car loan. The vehicle you drive is your bread and butter, make sure you are covered.

COMPREHENSIVE PHYSICAL DAMAGE

Comprehensive car insurance is usually overshadowed by its better known cousin, collision insurance, but it's just as important. Otherwise known as "other than collision" or "comprehensive coverage", the phrase is a bit of a misnomer. It actually doesn't give you complete coverage, contrary to what its name might indicate. Comprehensive car insurance really just covers damages to your vehicle not caused by a collision, and car owners can be surprised by how much this can encompass. Read below for examples of damages, and an evaluation of whether you need comprehensive insurance for your vehicle.

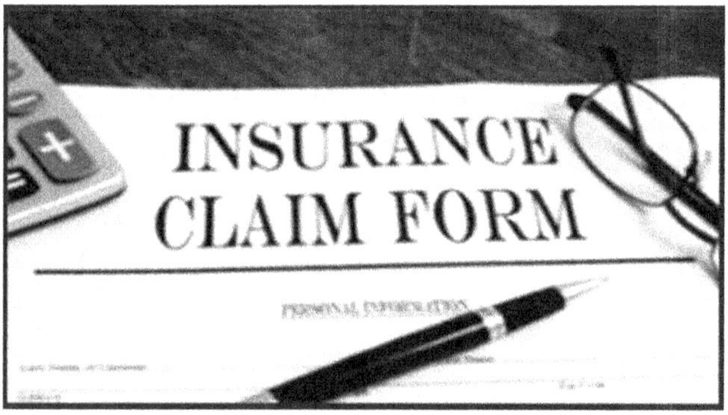

Talk to your insurance pro.

The key difference in collision vs. comprehensive coverage is to a certain extent the element of the car driver's control. Collision insurance will typically cover events within a motorist's control, or when another vehicle collides with your car. Comprehensive coverage generally falls under "acts of God or nature", that are typically out of your control when driving – a spooked deer, a heavy hailstorm, a carjacking, etc.

LIABILITY

Liability is a type of car insurance coverage that's legally required in most states. It pays for damaged property, medical care, and lost wages for other drivers and passengers if you're found at fault in an accident.

As liability coverage is required in nearly all states, so, too, are the coverage limits that come with it. Each state sets its own minimum limits (minimum maximums) that drivers must maintain on their car insurance policies. These minimums are typically expressed in a 3-tier system: 25/50/15, for example.

These numbers mean the following:

25 – The maximum amount (in thousands) the insurer will contribute toward injury related expenses per person.

50 – The total amount the insurer will contribute toward injury-related expenses per incident.

15 – The max amount the insurer will pay for property damage for each incident.

When you buy your policy, you won't be able to select limits below your state's legal requirements. But you can always set limits that are higher. Liability coverage generally breaks down into 2 main categories: bodily injury and property damage.

Commercial General Liability Insurance

This is not very expensive for the coverage that you get as compared to other types of insurance. In our area it runs about $400 per year and is paid in one lump sum payment. It is well worth the price.

Uninsured Motorist

Will coverage will cover the cost of anyone that does not have insurance and things such as hit-and-run accidents.

Deductible

In an insurance policy, the deductible is the amount of expenses that must be paid out of pocket before an insurance company will pay any expenses.

Deductibles are typically used to deter the large number of claims that a consumer can be reasonably expected to bear the cost of. By restricting its coverage to events that are significant enough to incur large costs, the insurance firm expects to pay out slightly smaller amounts much less frequently, incurring much higher savings. As a result, insurance premiums are typically cheaper when they involve higher deductibles.

This deductible is amount that you agree to pay, per claim or per accident. This amount will be subtracted from the total amount paid by your insurance company. Example of this is if the claim is for $500 and your deducible is for $100, you pay $100 and your insurance company will pay $400

Company Furnished Vehicles

Business auto policies do not extend coverage to employees and their family members if the company furnished vehicle is operated outside the scope of the employers permission or if the employee rents or borrows a vehicle on a personal basis which is not owned, rented or borrowed by the business. Individuals who drive a company furnished vehicle must make other insurance arrangements to protect against these coverage gaps.

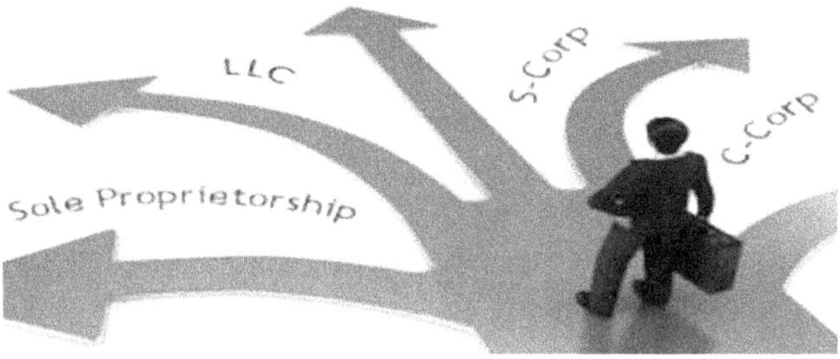

LLC. Is a choice that should be considered.

Umbrella Liability Coverage

This has a very large range and covers many things that are not covered in most of your business policy. These are a few of the areas that can be covered, but are not limited to just what is listed here: personal injury, advertising, blanket contractual, worldwide, liquor, drop-down, products and control.

This provides replacement coverage for underlying policies that have been reduced or exhausted by loss.

Earnings (Business Interruption) Coverage

Will provides loss of income coverage for your business by replacing your operating income during the period when damage to the premises or other property prevents income from being earned. There are a lot of variables with this coverage so be sure of what you are getting when you ask your agent for this type of coverage.

Product Liability

This covers bodily injury or property damage by the merchant or manufacture as a consequence of some defect in the product sold, manufactured or installed by the contractor which was the result of improperly performed work. What do they mean, exactly, by insured? Insured means that you are covered by commercial general liability insurance. This type of insurance covers things like property damage and personal injury. If you are working on a job and you make a mistake that causes someone to get hurt, or if you damage property, you will pay your deductible and the insurance company will take it from there.

Now, some states have different regulations and some insurance companies offer different kinds of coverage. Be sure you talk to your insurance agent about exactly what your policy covers. Ours will cover damage to personal property, "false" advertising (if I accidentally advertise something incorrectly), fire damage, any kind of medical expenses, products, installations that were incorrect, and so on.

Understand that "false" advertising and incorrect installations are only covered so long as I intended to be fair and honest, and only if I were not incompetent in our installations.

Workers' Compensation Insurance

Workman's Comp is a program that grew out of mutual agreement between employers and employees. In order for business to protect itself from being sued, an agreement was reached with the employee. This agreement was for an injured employee to get medical care for their work related injuries in addition to some form of compensation until the employee has recovered and returned to work. The conditions that would be covered under workman's compensation rely on a couple factors such as the injury came from a work related accident and the employee really is disabled. Many states have a state provider for this coverage and you may also go to your own independent agent to get covered. If you are a large enough company you can become self-insured and offer your own policies. The only time that you do not have to have workman's compensation is if you work by yourself and have zero employees. Keep in mind that subcontractors are considered employees and have to be covered or must carry their own coverage.

This insurance is mandatory if you have employees. The only time that you do not have to carry workers' compensation is if you work by yourself and have zero employees. Subcontractors are considered employees in most states and have to either be covered or carry their own coverage.

Bonding

What does bonded mean? Most car openings advertise that they are bonded and many customers look for this in your advertising. Most people think that in order to get a bond you have had to go through an extensive background check on your character and that only the elite: in both honesty and trustworthiness can get a bond.

A bond is insurance for your customer. It guarantees that money is available to reimburse your customers should you be convicted of stealing from them. In most states car opening businesses are not required to be bonded. It is simply an option that may benefit your business by bringing a sense of security to your customers.

It is very easy to get a bond in this trade. Fill out the order form that is in the trade magazine that you've purchased, send in the fee, and in about three weeks your bond certificate will arrive in the mail. There are no background checks, and nothing is required other than being a subscriber to the magazine. These bonds normally are a yearly fee based system based on a subscription and the expiration date. Each magazine has its own bond and they vary from a low of $5,000 to the highest (that I was aware of at this time) which is $15,000. The amount of the bond is the amount of money that is guaranteed to be available for reimbursement to your customers if you are convicted of stealing from them. The cost is very low, $5 to $15 per year

Chapter Five

Training & Education

Car opening training, unless you enroll in a campus course (full time day classes) which very few of us starting out can do, it is basically a self-educating process. Even the formally trained will become self-educating after graduation because the training never ends. You do not need formal training to open cars but car opening classes and seminars are available and may be helpful. If you subscribe to a trade magazine, you should know about these changes and how to deal with them. This is how you can keep up with the never ending changes of this trade. It is part of staying informed and being up-to-date.

Continued education in car opening is accomplished in very much the same way that many professionals continue their education. It is done through books, YouTube, online videos, newsletters, magazines, seminars, supplier sponsored classes, trade associations, trade shows, schools, correspondence courses, and relationships with other people in your trade. In this section we will take a look at each individual educational tool at our disposal.

Experience and Practice

OJT or on-the-job-training, under an experienced employer is the very best training you can get but it comes at a high price. You work long hours, nights, and weekends at lower wages. It also costs you your independence; you are working when someone else wants you to.

Books

There is limited number of books available to you in this field. The only thing you need to know about books on various subjects in this trade is where to get them. When you subscribe to a trade magazine you will find a list or two that you can order from right in the magazine. Your supplier will have a list of books for sale also. Some trade associations have a free library of books and videos available to members. These have usually been donated by other members. Books are timeless if you are in the middle of nowhere and you have your book or manual in the service van, just crack the spine.

Videos & YouTube

Videos and YouTube are fairly new to this trade but the number and kinds available are increasing. Many are free online and some are subscription bases services. Watching a video is just like having someone standing beside you showing you how to open the door. You will get a much clearer understanding of the subject being taught by watching a video, most likely you will learn quicker than by reading a book. Video and YouTube services are normally free but many are becoming pay per view and can be expensive. I recommend trying to get the free video or YouTube rather than the book, if the option is available. These forms of training is very effective but remember that anything you are learning should be considered theory until you have actually done the work yourself. There is no substitute for "hands-on" experience.

Word of caution about the internet and videos on the internet, these may or may not really work. As for the accuracy in them, so are very good, some are factious at best. Many are from beginners and want-to-be car opening experts and you could cause more damage than what you're being paid to do. If you are depending on the internet to pull you out of a jam and your lap top fails, what will you do? Learn the basic and built on those skills.

Correspondence Courses

These car opening courses allow you to study at home, almost all are now "online" and many will send you out study aids. These courses can be done at your own pace and are much less expensive than classroom study courses. Correspondence courses cost anywhere from $750 to $2,000. Almost all of them offer a payment plan that is very affordable and which makes these courses available to almost everyone. The completion times here are suggested times from each school but you can complete a twelve month course in three months if you want to study hard.

Magazines

Trade magazines are one of your least expensive forms of education and an excellent method of keeping up to date on new products, tools, service procedures, and techniques. Start with one magazine subscription and read each issue cover to cover. One magazine is all I have time to read but if you find that you have the time to read more, then subscribe to another one.

The National Locksmith - 1533 Burgundy Parkway, Streamwood, IL 60107, Phone: 630-837-2044

The National Locksmith
1533 Burgundy Parkway
Streamwood, IL 60107
Phone: 630-837-2044

Locksmith Ledger - 850 Busse Hwy., Park Ridge, IL 60068, Phone: 888-556-2272

Locksmith Ledger
850 Busse Hwy.
Park Ridge, IL 60068
Phone: 888-556-2272

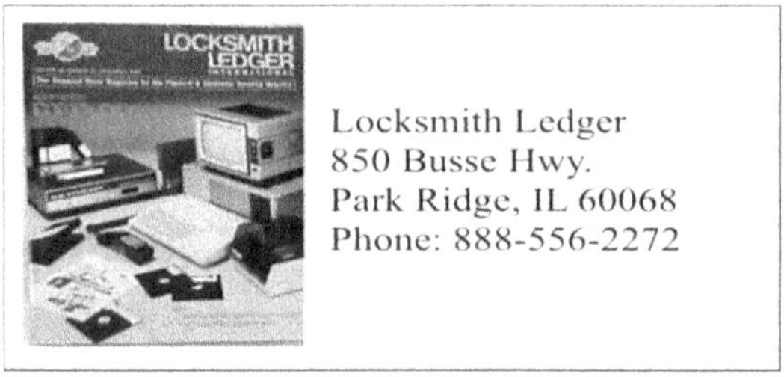

SCHOOLS

The schools for this industry changes every month so the is no list of schools in this manual. Just in case you are interested in getting some classroom instruction, search the internet for "Locksmith

Schools". I'm unable to give costs for instruction at each school but you can expect to pay from $2,000 to $10,000 (and higher) for classroom instruction. These costs vary greatly from school to school and some schools prefer to customize classes to meet your needs. This is much more cost effective for you. You may be required to take a test (for a fee) before you enroll to see where your weaknesses are and you'll receive counseling as to which areas need improvement. Most schools want to make sure you actually know, what you think you know, before training you in other areas. Some of these schools are correspondence courses and some offer classrooms "onsite" instruction.

Trade Associations

A car opening trade association is a group of individual car openings who have come together with a common desire to make the car opening industry better. They normally have monthly meeting and provide education, sales representative and their products. You have the opportunity meet with people of your same profession. These groups are about education, contacts and how to make the trade more enjoyable.

There is normally a yearly membership fee for joining the association which helps cover the cost of classes, the meeting room, supplies, newsletters, and so on. The association does not collect fees for profit and you will more than get your money's worth in education alone. This is also a great place to get referrals and help from other experienced car openings. The main thrust of most associations is to develop a "let's work together" attitude. Some of the car opening experts will only refer business to other members of the association in an effort to get more members to join.

When you join one of these associations you will be expected to adopt their "Code of Ethics" which basically is a "Code of Honor." This industry is an old trade; its secrets have always been guarded. You should be proud to be in this trade. Your customers must know they can trust in your honesty completely.

The list of associations can be found online. New groups are being formed monthly. Before you contact any of the groups on this list, check with a car opening expert in your area to find out if there is a local group in your town. Also find out which national associations the car opening experts in your area have a membership to. Be interested in their ideas and thoughts and ask questions!

Newsletters

Occasionally you will receive newsletters or emails from your suppliers letting you know about a new product or service they are offering or changes in company policy. They will also keep you informed on upcoming seminars and trade shows they are sponsoring. Trade associations send out newsletters once a month to everyone on their mailing list and most do not require that you join their association to receive their newsletter.

Blogs & Forums

These forums are full of all kinds of information. The best thing that I personally like about the joining a forum is that they keep me informed, several months in advance, about all the new procedures, tools and trade shows that are coming up. There is usually a good article on a service procedure, a new trick, or a tip of the month. Also, I find these forums to be more concerned with overall issues that affect our businesses, such as a new laws or policies regarding car opening and product installation. There are photos, stories, short cuts, methods and much more. Some require a fee other just want you to sign-up.

Seminars

Seminars come in a few forms; classes, webinars or lectures. They can be as short as two hours or as long as two or three days. Usually a seminar is a short three to four hour "hands-on" training class that your supplier has arranged to hold at his location during the evening (after hours between 6 p.m. and 10 p.m.). These lessons are on bypass methods or selling strategies of one product or product line.

There is a fee to attend these classes but you usually receive free product for attending. Occasionally a supplier will put together a weekend seminar that lasts all day Saturday and all day Sunday and offers a selection of classes for you to choose from. These two day seminars are held at local hotels and provide low cost training you should take advantage of these seminars. They are an excellent way for you to get to know your suppliers. You will be notified by your suppliers and through your local association newsletters of these upcoming seminars.

Trade Shows

A trade show is something like a car opening carnival. A trade show is a chance for manufacturers to show their products and try to sell you on the idea of selling their products versus their competitor. They will do many different things to entice you to come to the shows such as giving away door prizes and having free drawings for prizes during the show. These are sometimes very good prizes worth from $5 to over $1000. It depends on the size of the show. Some offer prizes or samples just for visiting their booths. Lunch is almost always a lavish buffet and free to everyone.

"JustCars" is the largest automotive trade show in the USA. You can visit them at www.justcars.us

www.justcars.us

Manufacturers, tool companies and everything that you can imagine that is even vaguely car opening related, can be seen at the larger shows. I have even seen spy products on display with factory representatives on hand to show you how everything works. Some of this stuff will really blow your mind! You'll walk away saying, "Man, I thought that stuff was only in the movies! "

Manufacturers set up booths so that you can walk around and look over their products and ask questions. You can be sure that there is probably no one who knows more about these products than the manufacturer's representatives. Some car openings (ourselves included) go to these shows, large or small, just to hang around and get to talk to some of these experts. You will be surprised at the questions you'll come up with when you're talking with an expert.

Most of the larger shows are put on by associations. One of the largest associations is ALOA. This group puts on a show once a year and is the biggest show that I have ever seen. It could take you three days just to walk around and look at every booth. It is held in a different town every year and usually lasts for at least a week. During this time classes are available all week long and the instructors are experts in their fields. You will find out when and where this show will be through the trade magazine you've subscribed to. Usually you will read about it at least three months in advance. When you see this show being advertised, you will need to call the advertised number to have ALOA send you an information packet which includes class information, discount airfare, hotel arrangements, and so on. If you decided you were only going to go to one show in your lifetime, this would be the one!

Relationships / Networking

Developing a good relationship with a few car opening experts in town is a good place to start. If you approach them properly, you can get them to train you. I see this happening every day in our town. A beginner shows up in town and wants to learn everything there is to know about car opening. He begins making friends with the other car opening experts and ends up being trained by not one but usually three or four different car opening people. Your approach must be handled in the following way to be effective:

- *Be honest, trustworthy, and dependable.*
- *Be genuine. Make him feel like he is the very best in his field, always say thank you..*
- *Validate that person's value as a professional.*
- *Never ask or assume that anything is free.*
- *Always offer to pay for his time and materials.*
- *Tell that person that you would feel privileged to be taught by him.*
- *Talk to them in person, no emails or no texting*

If you go about asking in this way, I don't know many people who would turn you down. Some will train you free if they know you consider them important and that you really care about learning from the best and doing the job right.

CHAPTER SIX

PAPERWORK

There are only a few forms that you will need to use in this business. I will be covering the basic forms that you will be using to run your business (excluding any forms used for bookkeeping) in this section. You may find that these forms are the only forms you will need to use. These are all of the forms that I use.

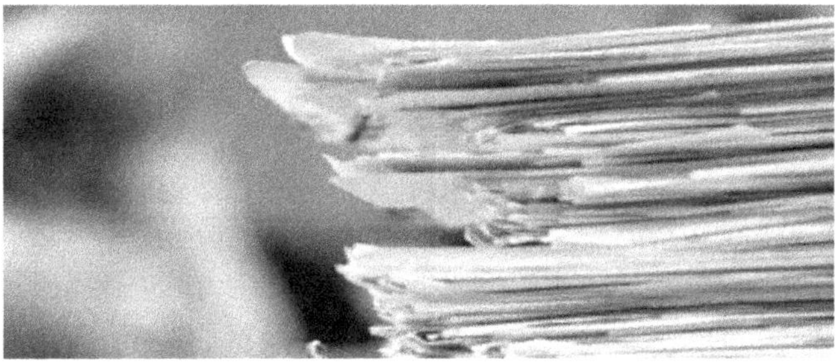

WORK TICKETS

Every time the phone rings you should be reaching for a work ticket at the same time you are answering the call. A work ticket is used to record the information you need to be able to go out and do the work. It can be a customized form that you have made at a print shop, a legal pad, a post-it note, or a piece of scratch paper. Always have a pen and paper on you for this purpose. It almost goes without saying that you need to do this. I will be covering the work ticket here because there is some specific information that you will need to collect that will make your job easier.

You should get as much of the following information as you can on your work ticket;

- *Name of the caller*
- *Person to contact at the job site*
- *Phone number*
- *Jobsite address/directions*
- *Quote or price estimate*
- *Method of payment*
- *Estimated time of arrival given to customer*
- *Time the call ended.*

Do not turn down a job because you cannot get all the information that you want. You will be surprised at the number of people who are not going to know exactly where they are, their telephone number, their address, apartment number, or even what kind of car they are driving. They usually know what color it is, but not always (no kidding). The more information you can get, the faster you will be able to complete your job and get on to the next one.

Many times a convenience store employee, hotel manager or shopkeeper will call for your customer. When this happens, your customer may not feel responsible for your fee if they did not personally request the service. Always ask to speak directly to the customer and have them agree to your fee before you accept a job.

Feel free to use any or all part of this invoice.

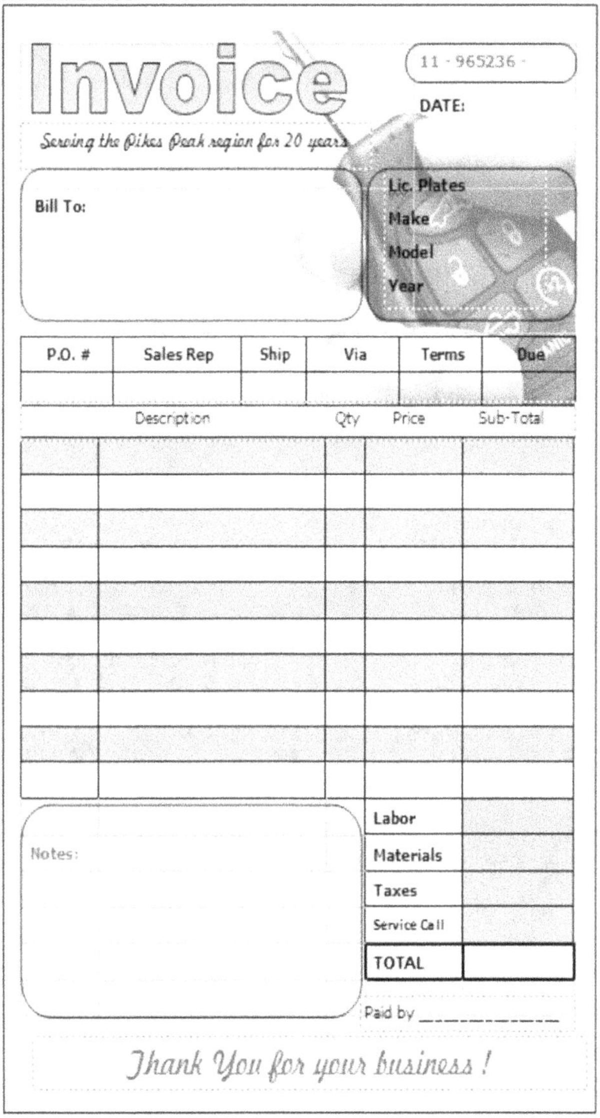

Invoice

11 - 965236 -

DATE:

Serving the Pikes Peak region for 20 years

Bill To:

Lic. Plates
Make
Model
Year

P.O. #	Sales Rep	Ship	Via	Terms	Due

	Description	Qty	Price	Sub-Total

Notes:

Labor	
Materials	
Taxes	
Service Call	
TOTAL	

Paid by ___________

Thank You for your business !

Your customers will only give you the information you ask for. You may arrive at the address they give you without knowing that you were going to find a large office building or apartment complex. If you have only asked for the address that is all you will get the building address. You don't want to have to spend thirty minutes trying to find your customer. You would expect that, if it was a large office building, your customer would tell you to go to the front desk and ask for them by name. If it was an apartment complex, you would expect them to give you the apartment number. The customer is upset and they will not remember to give you important information if you do not ask. Your customer will be waiting in an office or apartment for you to arrive and you will not know how to find them.

Method of Payment

Don't be afraid to ask what method of payment the customer will be using. They may be planning to pay you with a postdated check, out of state check, or a credit card that you are not authorized to accept.

I have opened many cars (before I adopted this policy) and had our customer say, "Okay, now you will have to follow me down to the ATM machine so I can pay you." This usually takes another thirty minutes of your time and the customer usually does not want to pay you for the time you are losing. Time is money in this business. Always ask what method of payment they will be using before you go to the job site. If they are going to want you to follow them to an ATM machine after you have opened the car, you will be able to quote a higher price for this service ahead of time.

Time the Call Ended

If you are running two or three lockouts at the same time you will want to know how long each customer has been waiting. A glance at the "Time the Call Ended" tells you which customer is next, if you are on schedule, and helps you plan how to handle any new calls.

AUTHORIZATION/RELEASE FORM

One of the more important items in the car opening industry is your "Authorization/Release of Liability" form protects you in two ways. The first item, the authorization, protects you from having criminal charges attached to you in the event that you have opened a car for a thief or any unauthorized person. When you require your customer to show a driver's license and car registration on each job, you can never be charged with negligence in the conduct of your business. You are, for all practical purposes, exercising "Due Care." Never complete a car opening without getting this identification. You will not be able to check the registration until you open the vehicle. If the registration does not match the driver's license after you have opened the car, it will be at your discretion whether or not to call a police officer and file a report.

The "Liability Release," potion should have many items on it. This is some samples that might be as follows;

> *I legally can and do authorize the work described below and hold bearer harmless from any resulting damage or claims.*

Make sure that you have these items on the release form also;

- *Customers Name & Phone Number*

- *Address, State, Zip*
- *Driver License Number*
- *Description of Work Completed*
- *Year, Make, Model & License Plate Number*
- *Method of Payment*
- *Customer signature, Date*

Authorization / Release; I hereby certify and authorize the work to be performed on this invoice/work order, vehicle, and/or security work. I further agree to absolve the locksmith/ service worker (s) who hold this authorization from any and all claims arising from the performance of such work. I also agree to pay any and all fees related to this work and agree to pay a return check fee of $250.

Signature____Date____________

Sample Authorization and Release

Authorization Part; The second most important item is a damage waiver that protects you from having to repair any damages that you did not cause. If you damage anything, you need to be responsible for it. On the other hand, if somebody tried to open that car before you got there, then you need to make sure that your customer understands that you're not going to be responsible for any damage done before you arrived. There have been many times that I have rolled up to a job and found clothes hangers sticking out of the window, paint damaged because of an attempt to wedge the door open, scratches on the window tinting, or broken molding.

There have been times when a security guard or police officer has tried using a Slim Jim tool (Slim Jim is a style of car opening tool) on a car that does not have any place for the Slim Jim, and will not work. Even though they are trying to help; they may tear up electrical wiring, break plastic parts, bend linkage, scratch paint, or rip the molding. If this customer does not notice the damage at that time, you may look guilty if you happened to the last person working on the car. It's important to know if there is any kind of damage anywhere on the car, you need to have the customer sign the release form first, and then you can open up the car. Explain to them, that if somebody worked on the car before you, you are not responsible for any damage they may have done.

Authorization / Release Forms:

These can be ordered from a car opening supplier or you can have your own forms custom made at a print shop using the sample. You can save money by ordering pre-made forms but you will eventually want to have this form printed directly on your invoices to cut down on the amount of paper you are handling.

Invoices

You can probably find a suitable blank invoice at an office supply store for use in your car opening business. This will be the cheapest way to start. As your business grows you should have your invoices custom made with your company name and logo on them to improve your professional image. The following checklist covers the important information you need to include on your invoices.

The sample invoice can be taken directly to your print shop. The printer can insert your logo and company information.

- *Information Needed on Your Invoices?*
- *Company name, mailing address, phone number*
- *Logo (if you have one)*
- *Date, Invoice number*

- *Name, address, zip code, phone number, job location*
- *Work ordered by, work performed by, terms, due date*
- *Description of work*
- *Authorization/Release*
- *Purchase order number, method of payment*
- *Quantity, unit price, labor, materials, tax, total*
- *Signature line to acknowledge the completion of work.*
- *Returned check fee, past due account fee*
- *Guarantee, Thank you*

Yes, you are going to spend more time filling out your invoice than it is going to take to do many of the jobs, but getting complete billing information is very important, especially with your regular accounts.

Are Invoice Numbers Important

Yes, and if you have a place for all of the other information on your invoice, then you won't miss any vital information. You may need that information in the future. If you have to call a customer back, you will know who to talk to. Invoice numbers will help you keep track of each lockout you accept and the IRS prefers that you keep track of each and every invoice. If one of your invoices is missing, the IRS may charge you taxes and penalties for the amount that the IRS will estimate was on that missing invoice, so keep good records to avoid the penalties and inconvenience.

You are encouraged to use any or this entire invoice;

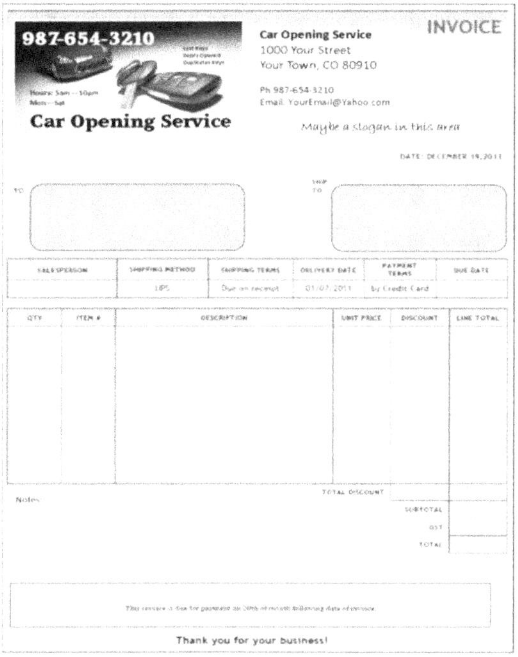
987-654-3210

Hours: 5am -- 10pm

Mon -- Sat

Car Opening Service

INVOICE

Car Opening Service

1000 Your Street

Your Town, CO 80910

Ph 987-654-3210

Email YourEmail@Yahoo.com

Maybe a slogan in this area

DATE: DECEMBER 19, 2011

TO

SHIP TO

SALESPERSON	SHIPPING METHOD	SHIPPING TERMS	DELIVERY DATE	PAYMENT TERMS	DUE DATE
	UPS	Due on receipt	01/07/2011	by Credit Card	

QTY	ITEM #	DESCRIPTION	UNIT PRICE	DISCOUNT	LINE TOTAL

Notes

TOTAL DISCOUNT

SUBTOTAL

GST

TOTAL

Thank you for your business!

STATEMENTS

Statements provide a summary of the work that you have done for customers who have charge accounts with you. Most of the time when you do lockout work, you will be getting your money right away. But if you get into the emergency road service work like AAA or Chevy Roadside Service, or if you work with car dealerships, you will not be getting paid right on the spot. These companies will insist on having charge accounts with you. This means you will be getting paid every 30 days (or sometimes 60 days) after the job is completed. For example, a roadside service company will call you and say: “I’ve got a job in your town. Do you want it?” The company will give you all the information you need to put on your invoice and when you finish the job you will have the customer (the person you opened the car for) sign the invoice.

There are a lot of little Emergency Roadside Service (ERS) companies that you may only do one or two jobs a month for. You can send those statements in right away. There are other roadside services that call me to do five or ten jobs a week. They don't want you to send them a bill every time you do a job. They want you to hold your invoices and send one bill at the end of the month. The roadside service company will pay all of the invoices listed on that one bill. Instead of getting fifteen or twenty checks for $30 you will get one check for $600. The ERS companies may require a copy of each invoice and they will want a bill that summarizes everything you have done for that month. When you work with these types of companies you may have to have a purchase order number on every invoice.

CONTRACTS

Contracts are not a form that you will use to run your business. However, since many people believe that I use contracts, I thought that this was the best section to discuss them. You are going to hear other car openings saying, "I have this contract," and "I have that contract." In reality they may have no contracts at all. They are telling you who their regular customers are. There are very few contracts to be had in this business.

If you tried to present a contract to a business they would probably laugh you off the property. A contract is a one way street: your customer's way.

When you're dealing with contracts, the contract won't be from you to your customer; it will be the opposite. The reason for a contract is because your customer wants a discounted price or a set price that you agree not to exceed. If they have a lot of work for you, they will want you to sign a contract saying that you will not charge them any more money than the amount on their contract. This means you may have to do after hours calls for them at your normal daytime rates.

CHAPTER SEVEN

MONEY MATTERS

This section covers all the different forms of payment you may be asked to accept and how to handle them. You will learn how to properly accept a check and how to collect on a bad check. You will get familiar with accepting charge cards, setting up and handling charge accounts, and using purchase orders. I will also show you how to set your pricing structure and determine how much you will charge for your services.

Money is why we work.

How Much? The first area I'm going to cover is how much to charge for your service. You can actually charge whatever amount of money you can get someone to pay. There are several ways to figure out how much you should charge for your service. The best way to start is to find out what the going rate is for the particular job you're doing in your area and then adjust up or down from there.

Do this by calling your competition and asking them how much they are charging to unlock a car door. If you let them know that you are the competition calling to check prices, you are not going to get accurate information. They may give you high prices in an effort to make you the highest priced car opening company in town or they may give you ridiculously low prices to discourage you.

Here's an example of how to make these calls. Give them all the information they want. Find out how much they charge and then say, "I'm going to call a couple more places, Thank You." It is important that you say this to avoid confusion and to let them know that you are not asking them to send someone out. You will want to set your pricing so that you are not the cheapest or the most expensive. Pick a price somewhere in the middle. It seems that the people who have the lowest prices end up getting a very high percentage of bad checks.

> *In Colorado Springs, CO. back in the year 1993 a lockout service was going for $30. I wanted to see if the customers would pay a higher price. This curiosity caused me to try charging $40 per trip to unlock a car. Back then that was a full day wages for the working man. I stuck to the higher price for years and received as much work as I could do. There is no "Real Price Ceiling" and this is why your efforts to find the going price are important. Don't use your "Gut Feeling" to make your lockout prices.*

There are other circumstances that affect pricing such as weather, special occasions, distance to the job, and holidays. At these times your prices should go up. If you are not sure what to charge during these times, just call your competition and ask how much they are charging. Pay particular attention to how many of them are not even answering their phones. If you are one of the very few services available, because others are not answering their phones, then you should be able to charge more for your service. Keep in mind that you need to be aware of supply and demand and not give away your service.

Most of the time when a customer calls you can quote a flat fee. There are times, however, when you will need to consider mileage. If someone is calling outside your normal service area, consider charging your flat fee plus $2.00 for each mile outside your normal service area. If you live in a rural area, everything may be based on mileage instead of a flat fee. This would depend on the area in which your business is located. Find out what your competition is doing and follow suit and don't be afraid of being the higher priced guy.

Another way to charge for your service is to charge a service call and an additional fee for the type of work you are doing. A good example is: $45 for the service call, plus $20 for every car door you open, yes there are times when a dealership screws up and you have to open several cars in one spot.

CASH

Cash is always the safest kind of payment to accept. There is no risk involved. All of the other forms of payment that you will receive are actually promises to pay. If you get paid in cash, then everything is done. Give your customer a receipt and the job is finished. Do educate yourself in what happen if you get counterfeit money, it happens, not very often but be prepared for that off chance of getting some funny money.

CHECKS

Checks use to be the most common form of payment you will be asked to accept. You are not required to accept anyone's check as payment for your service. If you accept checks you are going to get some bad checks that you will not be able to collect. I am to the point now where I do not recommend that you accept checks as a form of payment. Most everyone has a debit or credit card and checks are going by the way of the dinosaur. There is an exception, I do still except checks from business, but not from individuals. This decision is one you will have to make about running your business. Remember if you tell the people on the phone before you go to help them,

"I can take your credit card or cash, but we do not take paper checks anymore."

Guidelines for Accepting Checks; There are several guidelines you need to follow for accepting checks. These recommendations will help you decide which checks to accept, which ones to reject, and how to collect on the occasional bad check you have accepted.

Be Cautious of New Accounts; A very high percentage of the checks returned for insufficient funds are written on accounts that are less than one year old. The check number appears in the upper right-hand corner of all checks. Be very careful of checks numbered 101 to 200.

Many banks are now printing a date code on checks. This code usually appears near the address information. The date code is a three or four digit number such as "1297" which indicates that the account was opened in December 1997.

Require Two Forms of Identification; the requirement of a valid driver's license or an official state identification card is an absolute must for accepting checks. Write the license number on the face of the check along with any other information that is not printed on the check such as address and both home and work telephone numbers. Make sure that the license is valid, check that the person offering the check is the same person as in the photograph, and compare the signatures for a good match.

As second identification, the "Guaranteed Check Card" is preferable. Be sure to comply with the provisions mandated by the issuing bank. You will find these on the back of the card. Unless these procedures are followed, guarantee of the check is not

Place All Information on the Front of the Check

Writing information on the back of the check is useless. This information will likely be covered with bank and clearinghouse stamps. If the check is processed for prosecution and any part of the key information is unreadable, prosecution is very unlikely. Use the cross method, but be careful not to write over any of the printing on the face of the check.

- *Example:*
- *Driver's License Number*
- *Salesperson's Initials*
- *Credit Card Number*
- *Other I.D. or Phone Numbers*
- *Always Initial Checks*

Always initial the checks that you receive. Place your initials on the face of the check with the other identification information. If the check is used as evidence in the event of a bad check prosecution, it will be necessary to establish who accepted the check and, in turn, identify the issuer. If you cannot prove by your initials or an employee number written on the check that you accepted the check, prosecution will fail.

Checks are almost a thing of the past

Checks to Avoid

Counter Checks - A counter check is a check which does not have any information printed on it to identify the person issuing the check. There is no account number, name, address or any personal info added.

Starter Checks - These are temporary checks given to customers until their printed personal checks are issued, these are brand new accounts, so be careful.

Two-Party Checks - A "two-party check" is created when a check written to one person is endorsed by that person to a second individual. You would be the second individual in this case. Two-party checks may be good but, if the check is insufficient, collection is very difficult.

Postdated Checks - If customers ask to give you a postdated check, they are telling you that they do not have the funds in the account to cover your fee. A postdated check is a regular check except that it has been dated for some time in the future. This check cannot be cashed until that date. Chances are that if the customer does not have the funds now, there will not be funds to cover the amount of the check at a later date either.

Altered Checks - Do not accept checks that have been altered in any way. If a mistake has been made on the check, have the customer correct and initial it or write you a new check. Do not do it for the customer that is forgery!

Out-of-State Checks

Before you accept out-of-state checks you may want to ask your local district attorney if their office prosecutes bad check writers from other states. Many do not because of the costs involved. They may file charges on the bad check writer but will not take any action to pursue it. If this is the case in your area, you will need to decide whether or not you will accept out-of-state checks.

Traveler's checks

These are common in major tourist areas. They are always good. You won't get as many money orders and you will probably never receive a cashier's check for, your service, but treat all three of these like cash and don't be afraid of giving change. They are as safe as cash, but you should deposit them like checks.

Credit & Debit Cards

It will be a great advantage to your business if you accept major credit cards. There are many different kinds of major credit cards Visa, Master Card, American Express, Discover, Diners Club, Check, Debit Cards, and so on. There are no differences between these cards as far as accepting them as payment; you will process them all exactly the same way.

The more payment options you have available for your customers, the more customers you will get. Occasionally, the only reason your customer will choose your service over your competition is because you accept the form of payment that they prefer to use and your competition does not. Example: Not everyone accepts American Express or Discover cards. If that's the card your customer uses and you accept it, you have an advantage over the competition.

With the "old school method" of accepting credit cards you will need to have what is called a merchant account. Most people will tell you to look into getting one of these accounts through your bank. Banks normally charge a high percentage rate to do this for you and they are much harder to deal with.

If you currently have a Discover Card in your name you are automatically approved for a merchant account through Discover Card Merchant Services.

Discover Card Merchant Services

1-800-347-2000.

If you do not have one of these cards, apply for one. This is the absolute easiest way to qualify for a merchant account. There are many other merchant service companies in the yellow pages and you can find them under "Credit Cards." Some of them only require a credit report to open an account for you.

Square Up

This is a smart phone based credit card method and you do not need to have a merchant account to have one of these types of card payment systems. How it works is; you purchase an adaptor that plugs into your smart phone, then you download an "app" to except the credit cards. After this part is done you go online and open an account with your billing and bank routing information. Within a day or two your account will be set-up and ready for you to except credit or debit cards. The cost as of this writing is just shy of 3% or $3 for every $100 they pay you.

This is the best method I have found; oddly they are fairly new, many 5 years old as of the writing of this book. They are by far the best I have used in the last 20 year. There are no contract, no monthly fees; no statement fees just the 3%. Also they do not require a contract, the cost of the swipe pad is under $20 and you are not under any obligations to continue to use them, it's a win-win situation for the small business person. They are very much up-to-date with any and all the safety, laws, keeping you up and running. Both you and your customer will get a receipt in their email or instant messaging within a couple of minutes. Your money will be deposited in about 24 hours from the time you finished the job.

Whatever you do, this is a must have app, they have their stuff together; they are safe, up-to-date and are very secure… Yes, they are secure! I say this because of a friend that is in the same business as we are, signed a contract with a credit card processor that charges for equipment, higher fees, monthly service charges and they had to sign an agreement form for several years. By the end of their contract they will be paying thousands of dollars over and above the "Square App" small under 3% fee.

Charge Accounts

"I would gladly pay you Friday for opening my car today!" I have heard this many times and I have found it not to be true. I no longer give credit in this way to individuals. Extending credit to your customers will be entirely up to you and at your discretion. What happens is; they are in desperate need of your services today, but once they are in their car again the priority to pay you is no longer important. You lose twice, the time you spent opening their car and again chasing them for the payment. You're better off politely telling them you are busy and cannot help them. This may seem hard at first, but after you have played bill collector a few times, it will get easier

You will need to give credit to some companies and almost all of your larger accounts (AAA and Emergency Roadside Service are examples) or you will not get their business. When you are dealing with a national car rental company, for example, they normally are not allowed to make payments from their branch offices. In this case you will probably be getting the requests for service locally and then mailing your invoices to their main office, which could be out-of-state.

You will almost always have to give credit to car dealerships. I am careful not to offend car dealerships by demanding cash payment on our first service call, this is because they could become a regular account. It is very inconvenient for them to stop what they are doing and write you a check each time you open a car at their request. Usually they call you because they have a customer waiting to look at the car that has the keys locked inside. The salesperson wants to give all of his attention to the customer instead of taking care of your bill. Most of these places prefer that you send them a statement (statements are covered in the section on Paperwork) once a month for everything you've done that month. The best way to handle these accounts is to set them up on a "Due Per Statement" basis.

Per Statement Billing

Per Statement Billing works this way. Everything is due on the first day of the following month. That means, if you did a job on the first day of the month that invoice would be due on the first day of the following month. If you did a job on the last day of the month, that invoice would be due the very next day (which would also be the first day of the following month). To use this system you will send a statement that lumps all of the invoices for work you've done for your client in the previous month into one invoice. Do not put your regular customers on a 30-day account. By the time you discover that they are not paying their bills, your invoices will have overlapping 30-day due dates. It will be difficult for you to complain about your bills not being paid if all of them are not overdue. (A common excuse when this happens is, "Oh, I was just waiting for them all to be due which, of course, will never happen?") When you use the "per statement" basis you will know immediately if your bills are not being paid and you will be able to stop a bad account from getting out of hand.

I do not give second chances to accounts that do not pay our statements on time. If I have a hard time getting our money the first time, I switch them to a "cash only" basis and they will have to pay each invoice as the work is done.

PO Numbers

PO is short for Purchase Order number. It is normally abbreviated PO. Many times you will get a phone call and someone will ask if you will accept a PO. You need to realize when you get this call that, if you say no, you could be turning down a very large account that could be a good source of regular monthly income for your business. When a company is asking if you will accept a PO, in most cases, this is the only method they are allowed to use to make purchases. If you say no, they have no other option but to call your competition.

When someone asks you to accept a PO number (PO#, PO and Purchase order are all the same thing), they are asking you to accept this number instead of immediate payment. In other words, they are asking if they can charge something. They are also asking you to accept a number that will correspond to a written record of the purchase. This is not a guarantee that your bill will be paid but it is proof that the work was ordered. You will write this number directly on your invoice. If the bill is not paid you will have the PO# to refer to when you call.

> ***Short Story:*** *I had a friend work for a large car lot, it was one of the biggest in the city with thousands of cars, he work for them for many years. Over this period of time they short paid him a car ever once in a while. No big deal but over time it added up. He kept great records and always asked for the money they missed every month. Until one day it was enough. He contacted an attorney and by the time everything was corrected he received tens of thousands of dollars because of his due diligence. The car lot did this to every contractor they had working for them; it was their standard operating procedure.*

Ending Notes; I am not nor ever been a bookkeeper or accountant. I'm just trying to give you a basic idea of how the money side of things works. If you have any professional questions that you need to ask, be sure you talk to a qualified bookkeeper, and/or an accountant, or someone in that profession.

Chapter Eight

Appearances

This section will cover vehicle appearance and uniforms, what the general public expects of a professional, and what you should provide as a professional car opening expert.

If you think of yourself as a professional and dress like a professional, your customers will treat you like a professional. You will get more corporate accounts and have a better relationship with your customers when your image and your attitude say, "I am here to provide a competent, complete and honest service."

Your vehicle advertises who you are, what you do, and what kind of service customers can expect. In fact, most customers will see your vehicle before they see you. Their opinion of your ability may be based on how you maintain your service vehicle, both inside and out.

Be neat, be clean, and be courteous. It will pay off in many ways and when you least expect it.

Vehicles

You should use the personal vehicle that you currently own when you are first starting out. I recommend that you spend as little money as possible on your business startup. After you see that your business is working, one of the first things you will need to do is to make your service vehicle look like a commercial vehicle. Your customers will be expecting a commercial style vehicle to arrive. When you drive into a parking lot you want your customer to be able to see you right away. You do not want to have to circle the parking lot trying to find your customer. If you have to hunt for several customers in one day you will use up a lot of time you could have spent opening other cars. It can really put you in a jam if you have other customers waiting.

Some car opening companies use pickup trucks, pickup trucks with campers on them, utility vehicles, or small cars with signs on them. Is this a good practice? Any type of vehicle that you have will work when you are starting out. If the vehicle you are using has rust spots, dents, missing hub caps or molding, or needs to be painted, you will need to get these things taken care of as quickly as possible. Along with any repairs that you may need to have done, you will also need to have professional signs made for your service vehicle.

The ideal service vehicle for this business is a cargo van. This is a van without windows on the sides. Even the older styles can be fixed up and painted to look as good as new for a few hundred dollars. This is the type of vehicle that most of your customers will be expecting and watching for when you arrive. The area for signs is large and high for good visibility. The problem you will find with smaller vehicles is that the signs have to be small due to limited space and are so low and hard to see that your customers will have a hard time spotting you. Can you get by for a few weeks or a couple of month, yes you can. Just remember that the sooner you look like you're in business the sooner things will start falling into place

SIGNS

Signs and the appearance of your vehicle are very important. The quality of your service will largely be decided by your customer from the appearance of your vehicle. Sloppy signs and poor vehicle appearance will show that you are not concerned with pride and workmanship. This will also reflect on how your customer thinks you will care for his car. If you are driving a beat-up looking car with hand-painted signs, you will get that customer one time but you will not get his business again. He will call your competition the next time he needs his car opened. Repeat business and referrals are very important to your success.

Don't be cheap when it comes to having your signs made. The cost for having a professional sign made for your service vehicle win range from $50 up to almost any amount you can afford. If you cannot afford to have a professional sign maker make and apply the signs to your vehicle, you are better off without signs until you can afford to have them done right.

There will be times that you will have to allow your customer to ride in your vehicle or just sit inside to stay out of the weather. Sometimes the parking lot is so large that it will be easier to pick them up at the front door of main building and drive them to their car. In this short time your customer is evaluating you for the next time they need your service. Keep the inside of your vehicle clean at all times.

Uniforms

Your personal appearance is very important. This includes the way you dress, the language that you use, and your personal hygiene. All of these factors will count when your customer forms an opinion of your abilities. You need to look like a professional, dress like a professional, and talk like a professional.

Most of the car opening professionals that I see are wearing jeans and tennis shoes but most of them wear a uniform shirt that has the company name on one pocket and the service person's name on the other pocket. Not everyone can afford uniforms right away so at a minimum wear a nice shirt, clean pants, and do not look sloppy. You will get dirty throughout the day but you should start out fresh every day.

Whenever you see a person in a uniform, you get a quick sense of who they are and what they do. The members of a sports team wear their uniforms to say "I belong to this group." Police officers and firefighters wear their uniforms to say "I provide a service to my community."

Over View

If you are going to wear a hat or baseball cap, have your company name put on it. It is not professional looking to wear hats with other business slogans or messages on them.

Your language can affect the longevity of your business. If you use bad language when you speak to your customers or if you are continually politically incorrect, they may not use your service again or refer your company to friends and relatives.

Your appearance will not only affect the amount of repeat business you will get, it will also help you on each job. Say you run into a car that is very difficult to open. You are having a hard time. You are a beginner. You have not done very many car openings. If you look sharp, it will go a long way. Your customer will still think you are a professional even though you are just getting started. Why is this? It is because, you do not look like an amateur, newbie or a beginner. Looking like a beginner will cause people to have doubts, and you do not want to give your customers any reason to doubt your experience. Look the part. Be the part. You will make more money just because you look good.

One more thing, It is ok to stop take a breath and look in the manual to see if your opening the car in the most efficient manner. The fact is most people would like to hear that their car is a tough one and not every with a Slim Jim can open it.

CHAPTER NINE

GETTING BUSINESS

This is the most important section of your car opening Service Manual and is what makes this manual so valuable. No other car opening book tells you how to build your business in this way. Many years of experience and our observations of other successful car opening business are presented here. When you are finished with this section of the manual you will know more about this business than most (if not all) of the experienced car openings that you will be competing against!

By using the information here you will soon increase your business so much that you will have too much work. Most of the business building methods here are proactive instead of reactive.

> *Active means "doing something." The prefix pro means "before." So if you are proactive, you are ready before something happens. The opposite is being reactive, or waiting for things to unfold before responding. Think about winter cold season. A proactive person washes his hands and takes vitamins; a reactive person gets sick and takes cold medicine.*

Most car openings are reactive, not proactive. They depend solely on their yellow pages advertising or word of mouth to get business. They passively sit by the phone waiting, and hope that a customer will call. I have some news for you. The world is a candy store but, if you want the candy you have to go trick or treating'!

These are the secrets to success in this business. Apply the suggestions given here. Study and emulate the practices of proven success. You are sure to reap the same rewards!

Learn to Think Like Your Customer

Contrary to what your competitors tell you, paid paper advertising is not the first place people look for help when they are locked out of their cars. I strongly suggest that you have a good ad presence, but capturing your customers before they get to that point is what you must try to do. Once your potential customer is looking on their phone and has found the a generic car opening service or towing section on the internet, you are competing with every other car opening service, locksmith or tow truck driver in town. Most customers will only look at the first three pages of the internet. They will normally call three or four companies and, if they all have the same price, usually the last person called gets the job.

The most common complaint heard from customers is that would-be vendors and suppliers "They just don't understand our business." Learn what your big account need, not what you want.

Some of the resources people go through before they will call you are:

- *Call a car opening or tow truck company they have used before*

- *Ask for help from people close by*
- *Try to open the car themselves*
- *Call family members to see if anyone has an extra key*
- *Call the car dealership to see if they have a spare key*
- *Call the police for help*
- *Call the fire department for help*
- *Try to force open the lock with a screwdriver*
- *Look for a clothes hanger*
- *Ask people close by for recommendations*
- *Call roadside assistance or AAA.*

Then, if all of the above methods fail they will go to the internet looking for a tow truck driver or a car opening to open the car for them.

You want to get a potential customer to call you before they get to the car opening, lockout or towing section of the internet. If you can, this will dramatically increase our chances of getting the job. There are many ways you can do this and one of the more profitable ways is to become a Roadside Service Vendor.

Become a Roadside Service Vendor

Most new car dealers now have a Roadside Service programs included,

at no charge with a new car purchase or sometimes a used car purchased from that dealer. This is a free service provided by the dealer that basically covers any minor breakdown on the side of the road such as a flat tire, running out of gas, towing charges, or car opening services. Sometimes car buyers know this and can call roadside service themselves. Many times they are unaware of the service, and when they call the dealer to see if there is a spare key, the dealer gives them the roadside service number to call. Roadside assistance service is easy for the person locked out of the car. It's a matter of calling the 800 phone number. The operator asks the nature of the problem and dispatches an appropriate vendor to take care of the difficulty. The person locked out of the car does not pay for this service. It is absolutely free. The vendor then bills Roadside Service Company for the car opening expert fee.

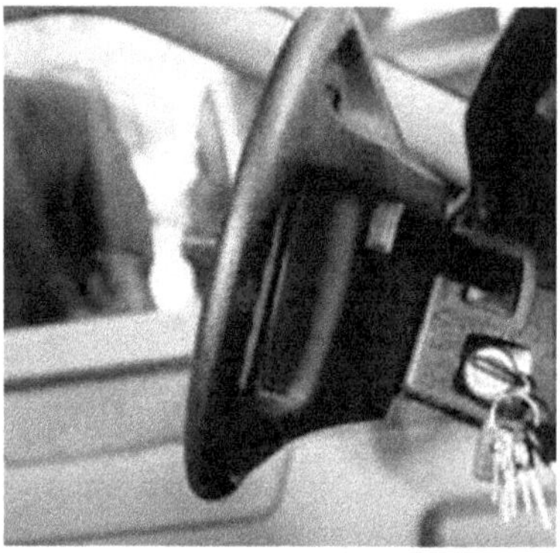

Insurance companies also provide this service for a small monthly/yearly fee to the insurer. There are two versions of this insurance. One is called roadside service and the other is called towing. Both of these are pretty much the same as far as your service is concerned and both will reimburse your customer for your fee.

From our experience it seems that the insurance companies are adding this service to all their customers without asking if they want to have it. The fee is small, about $6 for six months coverage, and if you tell them that you don't want this coverage they will argue that you need it! Should you complain that you have been paying for this service and did not want it, they will say they were doing you a favor! I believe insurance companies are making a lot of money by insuring many people without their knowledge, while people are paying for these roadside problems out-of-pocket because they do not realize they have insurance coverage.

If you will tell each potential customer who calls that their auto insurance may cover your fee, this will increase the number of jobs you get. Be sure to tell them that if they have this coverage there is no deductible to pay and that it does not affect their premium. The insured is normally allowed to use this service twice a year at no charge.

Roadside Service accounts can be very large. Just one account could be worth $25,000 a year or more depending on the population in your area. All you have to do is call the roadside service companies and ask them to send you an application to become a vendor. Each service may have different guidelines that you must agree to, such as being a 24-hour service and available 365 days a year, a member of the Better Business Bureau, able to meet their insurance requirements, and so on. Try to comply with whatever they ask of you. These accounts are worth any amount of jumping through hoops in order to land one.

Do a search on the internet for AAA, Roadside assistance, Allstate, AARP, 24/7… and the list goes on. Remember that the people trying to sell you this service needs companies like yours to do the work. So call them up and ask to be a service provider for them.

CAR OPENINGS

Your best sources for referrals from your competitors are going to be tow truck drivers, locksmith shops, roadside assistance services and other car opening companies because these are the two main sources of car opening services available to the public. You will actually get more referrals from the tow truck companies because there are usually more of them in town. You should stop by each locksmith shop in your town and introduce yourself.

SMOOTH TIP:

It helps to come bearing gifts such as donuts, cookies, or other goodies. Also call the locksmith's that are 'mobile only' and ask to meet with them for lunch or coffee.

It is very important when you are talking to a competitor, never to claim to be the best in the business or that you have better tools. You need to remember that you have fallen into the "gravy" part of this business and that most car opening experts have had to go through extensive training to be able to run their businesses. Some car opening experts may resent the fact that you only get the "gravy" jobs while they have to deal with the more tedious work associated with car and key business. You may be making more money than they are, don't rub it in. It will help your relationship to let them brag. All you need to do is show an interest in what they are saying and doing. For the sake of your relationship, when they ask you how your business is doing, no matter how much money you are making, always say, "Things have been really slow."

Try not to give the impression that you are only interested in what they can do for you; this will shut them out completely. You want to develop a relationship with them because both of you could profit from working together.

Start by explaining that yours is a new business and that you are a one man service. Next, ask them if they would be interested in taking any jobs that you could not get to if you are too busy. You need to develop relationships with several car opening companies so that you will have a backup system in place should you ever need help on a job or need to refer one of your customers to someone else because you get too busy.

You will get many referrals from the car openings in town just because most of them are on call 24 hours a day. Everybody needs some time off. They will refer customers to you at the end of the day and on weekends when they are tired or burned out.

Remember

There is only two times it not wise to brag about your car opening skills or your company when you are trying to get referrals. You already know when those times are: talking to tow truck drivers and talking to other car opening experts. This is sure to build rivalry between you, and they will not refer any customers to you. With everyone else it will help build confidence in your company if you tell them that you are the best in the car opening business. Tell everyone but tow truck drivers and car opening experts that you and your company are the very best, that you can open any car on the road quickly, that you guarantee no damage, that you can give a quick response time, and that you have very competitive prices.

The larger hotels/motels are more service oriented than the smaller ones and are a great place to “lock in” your customers. Most of the time when a guest is locked out of his car the hotel employees will take care of the problem for him. The person locked out will not even have to use the phone. Many times a guest will call the front desk and say, “I'm locked out of my car. Will you call someone for me?” No sooner said than done.

Many of the people working at these hotels/motels rely heavily on tips for extra income and taking care of problems like this is a good source for tips. You will need to make yourself known at the front desk and leave your card. You will also need to meet each bellboy, doorman, hostess, and server, and visit with every person on each different shift. Ask the front desk when the shift changes are and come back on each shift to introduce yourself to everyone all over again. Don't forget, someone else will be at the front desk. Hand out those business cards and leave extras for the personnel at the front desk.

If you can respond quickly and perform your service in a professional manner you will make these people look good, they will get more tips, and you will get more referrals.

Bulletin Boards

There are many free bulletin boards all over town where you can post a flyer or leave an index-sized card. You should use all of them. The best ones are at the supermarkets and larger superstores because they have lots of cars in the parking lots. Do not just post your stuff on the bulletin boards and leave. When supermarket and superstore customers get locked out they ask the store manager for help (or ask if they can borrow a clothes hanger). Always go into places and ask to speak to the manager. Everyone knows that these boards are open to the public but ask the manager for "permission" to post your advertisements. This is a good way to get to meet the managers and make them aware of your services. The next time they are asked to help locked out customers, they can helpfully refer them to the bulletin board instead of turning them away.

Security Guards

Security guards (for the most part) are seen by the public as police officers and they are asked to open cars just as often. Your best source for referrals from security guards is at the shopping malls. The security guards at the malls get so many requests to open cars that they have usually purchased a set of opening tools in order to be of service to the mall customers. I have never seen one of these guards with a good set of tools and their success rate is not very high. Shopping malls usually have a security office where the security supervisor stays, most of the time, to dispatch the other guards over a walkie-talkie system. The other guards are normally circling the mall performing traffic control, giving directions, and so on.

Start at the security office by handing out cards and telling everyone about your service. Try to talk to each guard and give each one your card. Do this during the day. If you are in the area late at night, drive around the mall and find the guards in the parking lot. This will be another work shift and you'll need to introduce yourself again.

Many businesses hire security guards to drive by and check their stores several times during the night. Look these security companies up in the phone book and stop by their offices to hand out your cards. You will soon begin getting referrals.

Car Dealers

Used car dealers will be glad to meet you and welcome you to their lots. They get locked out of their cars on almost a daily basis. They usually do not have spare keys and, between their salesmen and the customers driving the cars several times a day, they are sure to get locked out. Most of these lots already have vendors they use on a regular basis. You'll need to ask for the opportunity to be their backup just in case their regular vendor cannot get to them promptly.

Being locked out is usually an emergency situation in the eyes of the dealer. He is afraid that, if someone wants to look at one of the cars and it is locked, he will not be able to show it and will lose a sale. The dealer's main concern is how quickly you can respond when called. The very first time their regular vendor cannot show up on time you will have a new account.

This is such a good source for car opening business that almost everyone in our business visits these places trying to capture their accounts. You will have to be more competitive with your prices for car dealers. It won't take very many of these accounts to keep you busy.

New car dealers do have spare keys to their vehicles so only occasionally will you get a job or two there. Do visit the new car dealerships most of them have used car lots. If the salesmen at the new lots are impressed with you, they will often call the used car lot and recommend that they begin using your service.

Car lot accounts will come and go and will go back and forth between vendors. You will need to develop a close relationship with the salesmen at these places. These are the people who will be calling you.

KEEP THIS IN MIND:

Most car opening experts are only interested in developing a relationship with the managers. They think that this is where the business is. Wrong! It is the “little guys” who will be calling you.

Stop by whenever you are in the area and ask if there is anything you can do for them. This will help build your relationship.

Parking Lots

Anywhere that people are parking their cars is a good area to post your advertising or hand out your cards if there is someone close by. When someone gets locked out of his car he normally does not head straight for a phone to call for help. He will look for someone close by to ask for assistance. This is the trick to capturing your customers before they reach the yellow pages. Begin by looking for the larger parking lots that have at least 150 parking spaces. Some of these places will be department stores, shopping malls, hospitals, sports facilities, colleges, supermarkets, and large employers. Stand in the middle of the parking lot and look around. You are looking for places people will go to ask for help. If the closest place that you can see is a convenience store six blocks away, that is what you are looking for. There will normally be more than one place to go to where you could ask for help. Visit each of these places, hand out your cards, and ask if you can post an advertisement near the phone. At the smaller places you will want to give a card to each employee if you can. Don't forget to tell each person that you would like to be “Their personal car opening expert

Express Service Area

Purchase a fold out map of your town and circle the area around your "home base" or the area that you will be in most of the time when you are not out on a job. This area needs to expand out from your "home base" to an area you can respond to in fifteen minutes or less. This will be your "express service area" and this is the area you will want to saturate first.

Tell each potential customer or referral source in this area that they are in your "express service area" and you can respond very quickly to them. This will be a good reason for them to use your service. However, the main reason you are saturating this area first is to get more business in less time. You are not limited to an hourly wage rate of income in this business. The more cars you can open in an hour, the more you will increase your hourly rate of income.

If you can open three cars in one hour and charge $45 an opening, you've just made $135 an hour! This doesn't take place all the time but it does happen! I don't know why, but it seems that most of the time you don't get just one call at a time. Calls seem to come in groups of two or three.

CHAPTER TEN

TELEPHONE SKILLS

You and your telephone are about to become inseparable. You are joined at the hip. Your telephone has become your best friend, your worst nightmare, and your source of income. How you conduct yourself on the telephone influences your customer. Try to always remember that you are talking to a stressed and distraught person. Your customer is embarrassed, inconvenienced, and anxious in the best of circumstances. He may also be cold, hot, angry, frightened, late, very late, hungry, sick, or in trouble at home. You are a rescuer, a hero, and everything in life (at that moment) depends on you being able to save the day. Impressive! Now let's talk business.

Answering the Phone

Remember, you are a mobile service and you can appear to be a large corporation, a small mom & pop shop, or a fly-by-night con operation. It all depends on the level of professionalism you use over the telephone.

A very large part of your appearance is your appearance on the telephone. It sounds kind of funny saying "appearance on the telephone," but how you appear to your customers, how they visualize your company when you are on the telephone, is a very important part of this business.

Believe it or not, I've heard car opening companies answer "Yo!" These were not professional car opening people! If you simply answer "Hello," the caller begins asking himself these questions: "Do I have the right phone number? Am I talking to the right person? Did I dial the wrong number? Should I hang up and try again to see if I get the right company?" He may just hang up on you and go through the phone book looking for a different car opening company. If you answer professionally you will get a lot more business. Answer in a professional manner such as, "Hello, (announce your car opening service name)." Then say, "This is (your name); how may I help you?" or, "How can I help you today?" If you only answer, "Hello, how can I help you?" you do not appear as professional. There is quite a bit of difference between these two answers. One gives your caller the impression that you've answered another call, you don't want to do it, you're tired, it's late, and you just want to go home. The other sounds like you are saying, "I would love to help you, I'm ready to go!"

You need to have enthusiasm (pep) in your voice when you answer the phone. Do you remember the saying “People don’t care what you know until they know that you care”? Practice answering in the same tone of voice every time. Be enthusiastic, caring, and ready to go! I once worked for a car opening company that was very good at this and while under his employment I was required to ask customers if they had called around for prices and why they chose our company. You would be surprised at the number of people that told me “No, you did not have the best price but the man on the phone wanted our business more than anyone else!” Price is not everything. There is more to this business than having the lowest prices.

Reassuring the Customer

All of your callers have just locked their keys in the car. They feel stupid. They have to call someone they don’t know to ask for help and you need to make them feel comfortable. Never say anything derogatory such as, “Well, stupidity is expensive”, or “There are a lot of dumb people in the world.” If they tell you, and most of them do, that they feel so stupid for locking the keys in the car, you need to defuse those feelings immediately. If they are that embarrassed and you can make them feel comfortable they will be less likely to call someone else. We usually do this by saying, “Oh, I do that all the time” or “Everybody has to do that at least once.” It is not worth losing a repeat customer by offering someone who has used your service before “The Double Dummy Discount.” There are so many rude people in this business that if you act professionally the market is practically wide open.

Texting the Customer

This is becoming increasingly more popular, this is where your customer texts you for pricing. This is a new gray area and the best methods are unclear at this point. There have been times when I think it is a competitor checking my pricing as well as a real customer wanting service.

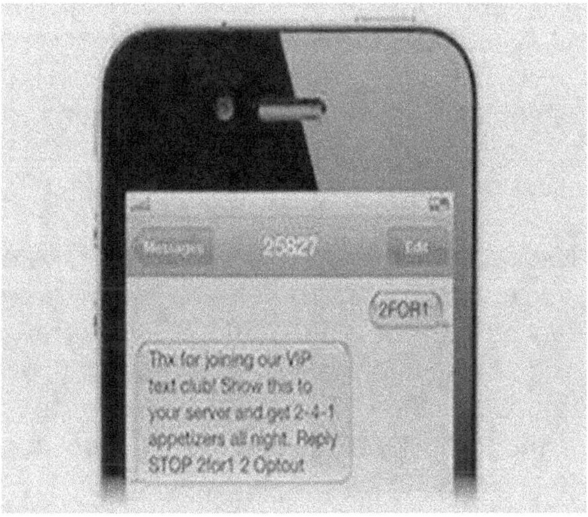

CHAPTER ELEVEN

THE LAW

It is your responsibility to learn the law. This means all the laws that pertain to your trade, and the way you do business, how you order supplies, and your liability. Learn local, county, state, and federal laws. Just knowing where you stand will protect you and your customers and will give you peace of mind. If you are on your way to establishing a good relationship with local and state law enforcement officers, you will find them a good source of information.

Nevertheless, learn the law. Don't take anyone else's word unless you are positive the information is accurate and current. Laws change, be sure to keep up on the latest information and protect your name and reputation. One of the best ways to protect yourself after you learn the law is to keep complete, accurate records.

Ignorance Is No Excuse

Both the court system and the IRS have adopted the policy of "Ignorance is no excuse!" and you will hear this almost every time you have to deal with them. "Ignorance is no excuse" means that you will not be given any consideration or tolerance in your sentence, penalties, or fines just because you were not aware that you were breaking a particular law or rule. As far as the law is concerned, as a car opening expert you are expected to protect the safety of the public and to exercise due care in the operation of your business. You are also expected to know what you may do and what you may not do in the interest of protecting the public as you provide your service.

What Is Due Care?

Sounds like "Do Care," doesn't it? Basically, as far as you are concerned in operating your business, this means that the law requires that you do care about the safety of the public you are serving.

> *Due care refers to the effort made by an ordinarily prudent or reasonable party to avoid harm to another, taking the circumstances into account. It refers to the level of judgment, care, prudence, determination, and activity that a person would reasonably be expected to do under particular circumstances. This standard is applied in a vast variety of contexts, whether the duty may be driving on the road or performing a background check. The precise definition is usually made on a case-by-case basis, judged upon the law and circumstances in each case.*

But just caring is not enough. You must show proof that you care. You must prove that you are only opening a car for the owner of the vehicle or other authorized person by obtaining proper identification of the person requesting your service. And you must keep a record of this in writing. Your Authorization/Release form will do this for you (covered in detail in the Paperwork section).

If you cannot get adequate proper identification you must use other means such as having someone else vouch for that person (and getting their identification), asking verification of identity from neighbors, the landlord, an employer, and so on. Always write this information on your invoice or authorization/release form.

Can You Be Criminally Charged?

If you were to open a car for a thief or other unauthorized person, could you be charged as an accessory to the crime? Unless the court is able to prove that you were negligent in the conduct of your business or had conspired with the thief or unauthorized person, no criminal charges could be filed against you. A car opening expert who requires all customers to show a license and registration or asks other persons to identify the customer before the car is opened is, for all practical purposes, exercising "Due care" and could never be charged with negligence in the conduct of his business.

> *Negligence is the failure to use reasonable care. Negligence may consist of action or inaction. A person is negligent if he fails to act as an ordinarily prudent person would act under the circumstances. What constitutes negligence will depend on the facts of each individual case.*

Postal Laws

According to the United States Postal Service, all car opening devices mailed in the United States are not allowed to be mailed through the Postal Service unless addressed to any of the following:

- *Bona Fide Car Opening Expert*
- *Bona Fide Repossessor*
- *Lock Manufacturer or Dealer*
- *Motor Vehicle Manufacturer or Dealer.*
- *Locksmith or Safe Company*

If you do not fall within one of the categories listed above, your supplies must be shipped via United Parcel Service (UPS) or Federal Express. It is unfortunate but, UPS is more expensive and takes longer to deliver than the United States Postal Service.

Possession Laws

It is the responsibility of the owner of potential “burglar tools” to ascertain and obey all applicable local, state, and Federal laws in regard to possession and use of these tools.

> *Burglary tool is an implement or a device designed to assist or help a person in committing burglary. Many states make it illegal to possess a burglary tool if the possessor intends to commit a burglary.*

> *A "burglary tool or theft device" can be any tool, instrument or other article adapted or designed for committing or facilitating a forcible entry into premises or theft by a physical taking.*

> *A person is guilty of criminal trespass if he knowingly enters or remains unlawfully in a dwelling, car or premises, or if he knowingly enters or remains unlawfully in a building, automobile or upon real property which is fenced, locked or enclosed in a manner designed to exclude intruders.*

It may be against local, city, township, county, state, federal, or other laws to own, use, carry, conceal, purchase, or have in your possession some or all of the tools necessary to perform your lockout service.

These include:

- *Lock picks*
- *Car Opening Tools*
- *Crowbars, Hammers*
- *Glass cutting equipment*
- *Any other tool used to commit a burglary*

Possession of potential "burglar tools" can be used as evidence against you if you are found in incriminating circumstances. An example of a state law to this effect can be found in the Virginia State Code: Section 18.2.94, Possession of burglarious tools, etc.

> *"If any person has in his possession any tools, implements or outfit, with intent to commit burglary, robbery, or larceny, upon conviction thereof shall be guilty of a Class 5 felony."*

Note that the prosecution has to prove intent. However the law continues,

> *"The possession of such burglarious tools, implements or outfit by any person other than a*

> *licensed dealer (these would include, Car Opening Expert, Repossessor, Locksmith, Lock Manufacturer or Dealer, Motor Vehicle Manufacturer or Dealer) shall be prima facie evidence of an intent to commit burglary, robbery or larceny."*

This means that the possessor of such tools may have a bit of a problem, to say the least, in trying to convince a jury that this "prima facie evidence" is misleading.

Since you are going to be a car opening expert you won't have any problems with possession of these tools as long as you can avoid incriminating circumstances. You must do this at all costs. A criminal act that would have been a misdemeanor becomes a felony if you are a car opening expert. Also you would be out of business instantly and you would have many car opening experts very angry that you disgraced and damaged their trade. One bad apple in this trade does affect us all. The ramifications are almost endless.

Relevant laws can be dealing with burglary, motor vehicles, car opening regulation, and so forth. A law in the state where I live can be completely different from the laws in the area where you live. It is important that you find out what the laws are for your area and determine the applicability to your circumstances (e.g., car opening expert, full or part-time, repo man, etc.) Find Out the Laws

It is important that you find out what the laws are for your area. You can probably find this information by calling your local district attorney's office or other law offices in your area. Begin by calling your state attorney's office and ask for a copy of the rules and regulations for operating a car opening business.

Quick Fact: Verifying the Model Year

VIN (Vehicle Identification Number) - The tenth digit from the left is by far the most referenced, it is the year manufacturer. This is important when the customer is not sure of the year made and the opening method is not the same. The VIN# seen in the windshield (Drivers Side) is the most reliable.

Code Year	Code Year	Code Year	Code Year
A ---- 1980	L ---- 1990	Y ---- 2000	A ---- 2010
B ---- 1981	M ---- 1991	1 ---- 2001	B ---- 2011
C ---- 1982	N ---- 1992	2 ---- 2002	C ---- 2012
D ---- 1983	P ---- 1993	3 ---- 2003	D ---- 2013
E ---- 1984	R ---- 1994	4 ---- 2004	E ---- 2014
F ---- 1985	S ---- 1995	5 ---- 2005	F ---- 2015
G ---- 1986	T ---- 1996	6 ---- 2006	G ---- 2016
H ---- 1987	V ---- 1997	7 ---- 2007	H ---- 2017
J ---- 1988	W ---- 1998	8 ---- 2008	J ---- 2018
K ---- 1989	X ---- 1999	9 ---- 2009	K ---- 2019

Chapter Twelve

Tools

The tools you see below are manufactured by

Pro-Lok
655 N. Hariton St,
Orange, CA 92868.
Phone 714-633-0681,
website www.pro-lok.com

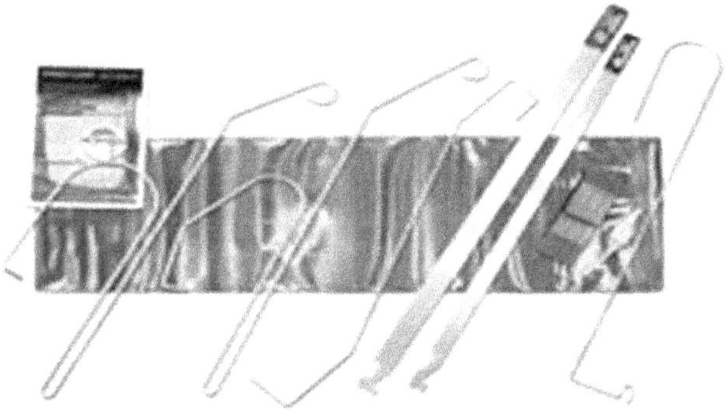

The above (SKU: AK04) kit is just under $100 and the below kit (SKU: AK42-Mega) is near $75.

The kit (SKU: AK42-Mega) is the first set you should purchase if your budget is limited. Then supplement your tools with (SKU: AK04) kit. Both kits are important and at some point you should have both.

The only other item would be the manuals that go with these two items. The manuals (5 Volumes) will let you open practically any domestic or foreign car door with ease. Pro-Lok also has an online service that will give you instructions for these tools.

If you look online your choices will be many, almost to the point of mind boggling. Stick with the proven methods at first then expand into some of the lesser used tools after your familiar with the tools you have.

This may sound over simplistic but to start use a real (paperback) book. If you depend on an online service and the service is gone down, your battery goes dead; your book will still be useable.

Basic Opening

One true fired way that even the Fire Department uses to open cars is the "Long Reach Tool" This is becoming the standard of the industry and most large kits that supplier would love to sell you are out dated on 90 percent of the cars on the road today.

The steps are quite simple: using a plastic wedge you pry the top of the door just enough to slide it the air wedge. Once this air wedge is in place, remove the plastic wedge and inflate the air wedge by squeezing the hand pump. You only need enough space near the top of the door to be able to fit the long reach tool into the crack of the door. This maybe 1/4 inch at the most, less is better. Then slide the long reach tool into the car and push the unlock button with the long reach tool. Once it's unlocked open the door and you are finished.

See illustration below:

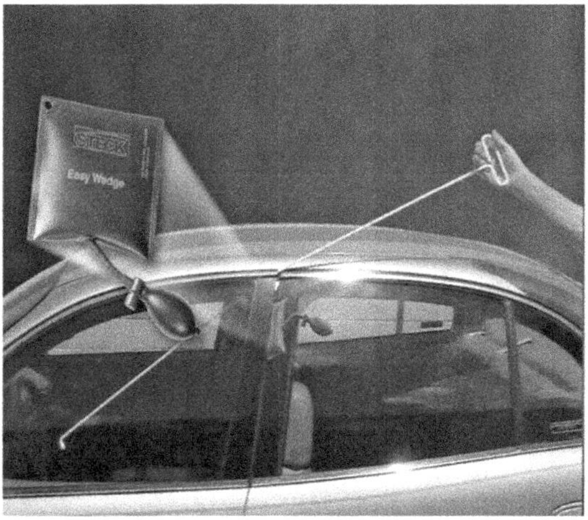

Word of caution: You are solely responsible for any damage you may cause, be it intentional or not. So be carefully and buy the tools that will cause little or no damage, all tools should be plastic or have a plastic covering to minimize scratches. Cold weather as well as hot can and will cause glass breakage. If you pull, wedge, grab, pry etc. This can and will bend the door or window areas of the car. Be sure you have insurance to cover any mistake that happen. Always work on the passenger side of the car.

SUPPLIERS

Support your local suppliers, it will pay in the long run!

LockPicks.com (Supplier)
1750 Rogers Ave
San Jose, CA 95112
info@LockPicks.com
1-800-539-2526
www.LockPicks.com

H.L. Flake (Supplier)
5235 Glenmont Dr
Houston, TX 77081
customer.service@hlflake.com
1-800-231-4105
www.HLFlake.com

HE Mitchel (Supplier)
www.hemitchell.com

Locksmith Ledger (Magazine)
www.LocksmithLedger.com

The National Locksmith (Magazine)
www.thenationallocksmith.com

This is just a very small number of suppliers.

Manufacturers Index (WMI)

VIN# Example – **2**G1FP22K6T2104553

The first digit represents the country of origin. So in this case the vehicle was built in the USA.

1 or 4 = USA
2 = Canada
3 = Mexico
J = Japan
K = Korea
E = England
W = Germany
Z = Italy

VIN# Example – 2**G**1FP22K6T2104553

The second digit represents the manufacturer code.

A = Audi & Jaguar	B = BMW
4 = Buick	6 = Cadillac
1 = Chevrolet	C = Chrysler
B/D = Dodge	F = Ford
7 = GM Canada	**G = General Motors**
L = Lincoln	D = Mercedes Benz
M = Mercury	N = Nissan
3 = Oldsmobile	2/5 = Pontiac
P = Plymouth	8 = Saturn
T = Toyota	V = Volkswagen & Volvo

Verifying the Model Year

VIN (Vehicle Identification Number) - The tenth digit from the left is by far the most referenced, it is the year manufacturer. This is important when the customer is not sure of the year made and the opening method is not the same. The VIN# seen in the windshield (Drivers Side) is the most reliable.

VIN# Example – 2G1FP22K6T**2**104553

Code Year	Code Year	Code Year	Code Year
A ---- 1980	L ---- 1990	Y ---- 2000	A ---- 2010
B ---- 1981	M ---- 1991	1 ---- 2001	B ---- 2011
C ---- 1982	N ---- 1992	**2 ---- 2002**	C ---- 2012
D ---- 1983	P ---- 1993	3 ---- 2003	D ---- 2013
E ---- 1984	R ---- 1994	4 ---- 2004	E ---- 2014
F ---- 1985	S ---- 1995	5 ---- 2005	F ---- 2015
G ---- 1986	T ---- 1996	6 ---- 2006	G ---- 2016
H ---- 1987	V ---- 1997	7 ---- 2007	H ---- 2017
J ---- 1988	W ---- 1998	8 ---- 2008	J ---- 2018
K ---- 1989	X ---- 1999	9 ---- 2009	K ---- 2019

About the author

S. Cormier, Car Lockout Business

I became a car opening expert from a slightly different background. I was a lot like most people that I knew. I had a dead end job and I was going no place very fast. I had set a goal to become self-employed at some time in my life, but things did not happen quite as fast as I thought. Here is how I started in the car opening industry.

In the early '70s I jumped from job to job trying to find some type of work that was satisfying and paid well. Money was important but if the job was too boring money did not seem to matter as much. Every time I found a satisfying job, the pay would not support my needs.

Then things started to change for me about twenty years ago. I started with a company that sold hardware to all the local hardware stores and car opening shops in the state of Colorado, and one of the product lines was keys. Over time I became acquainted with many of the car opening experts in my area by going into their shops to sell them keys. This, in itself, was not the miracle cure for the monotonous jobs. What it did do was show me the some of the ins and outs of car opening.

Being persistent, I finally gathered enough information to become more and more interested in this great opportunity of car opening business. I decided to get more familiar with the idea of working as a car opening expert and ordered a correspondence course through the mail. It took two months to get the courage to quit my regular job, although there was a little outside encouragement, money, free time, and no boss. Plus the fact that downsizing of the company that I worked for was also big help. I should thank that company. With the company in the slumps I needed a new job, and this gave me the opportunity to become self-employed.

I kept seeing car opening experts making lots of money and doing very little to get it. This is how I came to the realization that you can make a very good living being a car opening expert. Keep in mind that I followed the steps in this manual even though they were not in writing. The different sections of this book come from the experiences I have every day and I learned each and every part these hard way.

Are you wondering if I am a car opening expert? The answer is yes; I am and will be for a long time to come. This is the best career I've ever had and that's one reason why you should consider this opportunity very seriously. Enjoy the money, the extra time, and the freedom. I was forced into this career change by circumstances; but if I had had a manual like this one, the choice would have been a simple one from the very start.

Good luck, S. Cormier, Car Opening Expert

Index

AAA Colorado Headquarters, 7
Accountant, 49
Advertise, 52
Advertising, 14, 40, 51, 61, 65, 67
Answering Services, 70
Answering the Phone, 133
Appearances, 15, 48, 114
Authorization, 95, 96, 97, 138
Basic Opening, 144
Better Business Bureau, 123
Billing, 111
bonded, 22, 40, 56, 79
Bonding, 79
Bookkeeper, 49
Books, 44, 82
Bulletin Boards, 126
Business Card, 40, 56
Business Cards, 53
Business hours, 56
business name, 19, 28, 29, 30, 31, 32, 34, 41, 48, 69
Call Yourself, 19
Caller ID, 70
Car Dealers, 20, 128
Cash, 103
certified, 22, 56
Charge Accounts, 110
Checks, 104, 105, 106, 107
choose a name, 28, 30
Collision, 73, 74
Communications, 14, 40, 68
Contracts, 99, 100
Courses, 83
Customer, 48, 95, 120, 134, 135
Customer Base, 48
DBA, 32, 34
Debit Cards, 107, 108
Deductible, 76
Department of Revenue, 35, 36
Direct Mail, 63
Discount Coupon, 56
Discover Card, 108
Due care, 137, 138
Due Care, 95, 137
Education, 81
Emergency Road Service, 7
Express Service, 130
Firefighters, 20
Flyers, 63
Forums, 86
GEICO, 7
Getting Business, 15, 48, 119
Good Sam, 7
Identification, 105, 142, 148
Insurance, 10, 40, 72, 73, 75, 78, 122
Insurances, 14
insured, 22, 40, 56, 78, 79, 123
Introduction, 9
Invoice, 97, 98
Invoices, 97
JustCars, 88
Law, 49, 136
Laws, 136, 139, 141
Liability, 74, 75, 77, 78, 95
license, 24, 25, 26, 36, 37, 38, 95, 105, 138
License, 24
Magazine, 146
Magazines, 83
Magnetic cards, 58
Manufacturer, 21, 139, 140
Money Matters, 15, 46, 101

Networking, 67, 89
Newsletters, 86
order your tools, 21
Paperwork, 15, 46, 91, 111, 138
Parking Lots, 129
Patent and Trademark, 36
Payment, 94, 95
Permit, 24
Phones, 60, 68
PO Numbers, 112
Police, 20, 21, 117
Postal Laws, 138
Purpose of manual, 11
Radio, 66
referral, 29, 67, 130
Referrals, 67
regulating the trade, 22
regulations, 24
Release Form, 95
Repo Man, 20, 21
rewards, 55, 120
Roadside Service, 99, 110, 121, 122, 123
Rolodex, 58
Sales Tax, 36, 37
Schools, 84
Security Guards, 127
Seminars, 87
Signs, 65, 116
social media, 31, 32, 52, 61
Square Up, 109
Statements, 99
Suppliers, 49, 146
Tax License, 34, 36
Telephone, 16, 49, 132
Telephone Skills, 16
The Law, 16
theft device, 139
Tools, 16, 44, 140, 143
Top 10 Reasons, 8
Tow Truck, 20
Trade Associations, 49, 85
Trade Name, 34, 35
Trade Shows, 87
Training, 15, 81
Training & Education, 15
Traveler's checks, 107
Uniforms, 117
Vehicle, 21, 65, 139, 140, 142, 148
Vehicles, 76, 114
Videos, 82
VIN, 142, 147, 148
Work Tickets, 91
Yellow Pages, 17, 61
YouTube, 44, 52, 61, 81, 82

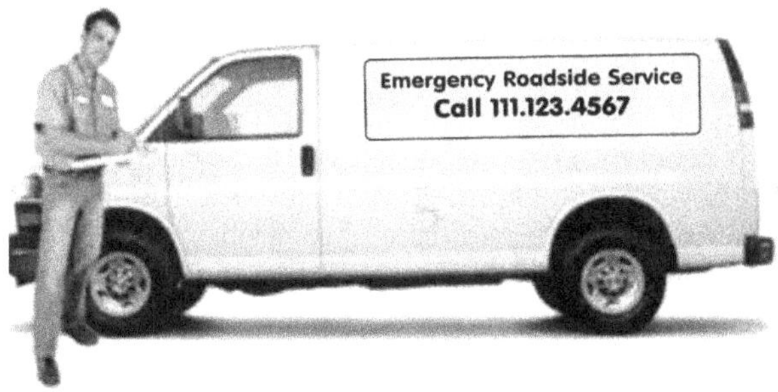

This is not a book that shows you how to open cars but instead shows what you need to know, what you need to have, and how you get yourself up and running so that you can make money.

ISBN: 9781790421619

Published by:
aDuxpond Publishing

ISBN: 9781790421619

www.ingramcontent.com/pod-product-compliance
Lightning Source LLC
Chambersburg PA
CBHW071310220526
45468CB00001B/317
9781790421619